THE FIFTH DOWN

(Football Thoughts and Other Things)

THE FIFTH DOWN

(Football Thoughts and Other Things)

by

Chuck Mills

Copyright © 2000, 2001 by Chuck Mills

All rights reserved. No part of this book may be reproduced, stored in a retrieval system, or transmitted by any means, electronic, mechanical, photocopying, recording, or otherwise, without written permission from the author.

ISBN 1-58500-453-7

This book is printed on acid free paper.

About the Book

"THE FIFTH DOWN is a terse, and yet comprehensive, gathering of highly individualistic, and often philosophical or provocative maxies, about football, winning, teamwork, life and 'other things.' Be it a sentence or paragraph, Chuck Mills shows great talent for saying meaningful things in a concise and memorable manner. Here is a highly personal document containing the essence of the author and his football career. It's warmth, humor and perceptions make it a great book."
-Rutledge Press

Dedication

To Barbara, who allowed me to chase my dream and have the chance to live it. To those coaches who assisted me in my career pursuits. To all coaches and their families, in all sports and at all levels, who have sacrificed to impact the lives of those in their care.

About Chuck Mills

Chuck Mills' coaching journey began with a grammar school team; then high school; small college, large university, private colleges, state schools and professional football. He was an assistant with the Kansas City Chiefs in Super Bowl I. His career as a college head coach spans five decades. He has received numerous coaching awards; had nationally ranked teams, and has been dismissed for losing. For over a quarter century he has been involved in the development of college football in Japan. He is regarded as the "father of modern Japanese football," and the Japanese equivalent of the Heisman Trophy is named for Mills. Off the sideline for eight years, serving as Director of Athletics at the United States Coast Guard Academy, for the 1997 season Mills added the head football coaching task to his portfolio. A team picked to place near the bottom of the Freedom Football Conference won the championship outright with a 6-0 record and finished the regular season with a 9-1 mark. That is the most wins ever in a regular season for the Academy. The team qualified for the NCAA post-season playoffs. The team was voted #1 in the final New England Division III poll. Mills was selected as the conference coach of the year; the Boston Gridiron Club coach of the year, and the AFCA/GTE regional coach of the year. He was also selected as a coach for the USA III College All-Star Classic. In 1998 the All American Football Foundation awarded Mills their Lifetime Achievement Award for football coaching and in 1999 the same award for athletic administration. Also in 1999 Mills was awarded the U.S. Department of Transportation's Superior Achievement Award, the highest award the department can bestow upon a civilian. He has also been nominated for inclusion in the College Football Hall of Fame.

Introduction

What follows are assorted thoughts about the game of football and other things. And the "other things" can be related in some way to football. Maybe very indirectly, but they can be applied to the game. These thoughts are in no specific order. Just one, then another.

Through the years things are read, heard, and created. Many have to do with life, society, integrity, and morality. All the things we say are a part of football.

Football is a great game. It isn't easily understood nor is it a simple thing to explain. But above all of this, there is the relationship that exists between coach and coach, player and player, and player and coach. It is said it is "only a game." For whatever the reason, it is more than a game. This book will not attempt to justify either position. What it will try to do is just pass along some thoughts about the game itself and the human condition in general.

This book was put together with the idea of providing some thoughts on football as well as other matters in the scrimmages of life. It intentionally goes from thought to thought without continuity. It was also constructed so the reader can pick it up or put it down with ease.

Redundancy emerges here and there. In coaching this is considered essential to having a team that executes well. . .in coaching it is called repetition.

It would be presumptuous to put these thoughts forward as original. Even those the writer regards as such, assuredly somewhere along the way another planted the idea.

It is hoped there will be a thought or two the reader will find interesting and may give some additional thought.

THE FIFTH DOWN

1st Down --- 1

2nd Down -- 65

3rd Down --- 129

4th Down --- 177

5th Down --- 255

The First Down

"In the beginning. . . .and the seventh day was rest." (Genesis) The seventh day may have been Friday night, Saturday or Sunday. Whatever the day, it must have been for Football.

***

Perfection, in or out of Football, is a goal seldom achieved. It is a goal, something for which to strive. In Football the effort is to control the imperfections as much as possible. The language to translate the control of the imperfections is called statistics.

***

Statistics are the result of human performance and not the other way around. The norm for acceptable statistics is derived from a long study of human performance. Humans create statistics; statistics do not create humans. When the human element is gone, we will have an exact science and the game of football will cease to be a game for people.

***

In recruiting there are certain colleges who are selectors. They pretty much can attract whomever they want for their football program. Their problem is not as much "what good players can we attract," but more a case of making sure they select the best of the pool afforded to them. The other colleges are true recruiters, trying to sell their programs to player and parent and emerge on top in recruiting against other colleges in a similar situation.

***

An observation, if not a statistical fact: it seems that in the recruiting wars, if a recruited athlete must change planes to reach a campus, there is little chance he will enroll. The airport layover seems to have a negative effect. It makes the college seem remote, and access to it cumbersome.

***

Beware the local athlete. There is always pressure to recruit the local youngster. It is good public relations and a great solidifier of local support. But beware! Be sure, in your projection, the player will be at least a two year starter. The local lad who doesn't pan out presents many problems to the program.. The player and the family are usually far more upset than if the youngster was a distance from home. The situation locally, is lived with every day. The player and his family are known and every day something is said to cause unhappiness. The lad just can't get lost. If there is any doubt about his ability then it is best to question taking him. It may be better to have him go elsewhere and star than come close to home and not play. It is much better to have people say you "blew one" and are a dummy, than to have him home and in an embarrassing situation for him and harassment for you.

***

The secret to successful football staff relations is the ability to "not get along." Coaches are highly competitive people in a very high profile and high pressure business. There is no way disagreements will not take place. The coaches must be mature enough and be pliable enough to understand this and when differences are heatedly voiced, the next day the coaches must start fresh. Harbored resentments fester; sides are taken, and soon the staff is divided and this division is easily communicated to the players.

***

Objective evaluation of prospects for the coming season to be understood and accepted by the program's supporters is a luxury reserved for the off-season only. When the season starts..these realities evaporate: only the scoreboard matters.

***

Be it group meetings or one on one, it is important that both parties fully understand the conclusions of the meeting. We often hear something differently than what is intended. The supervisor of the meeting can save future misunderstandings by briefly summarizing the meeting in writing and distributing it to the participants. This should have all the parties on the same "wave length."

***

We often neglect the power of public opinion. Often the majority does not participate in creating public opinion. They are content and silent. It may be assumed public opinion is what the vocal minority say it is.

***

A great example of the power of public opinion was the sweeping visit the Pope made through eastern Europe in 1979. The Soviet Union and its captive countries with all their power over the masses, were helpless in thwarting Pope John Paul II from speaking and drawing crowds; nor could they stem the massive expression of faith by the masses.

***

It seems in countries ruled by the majority, the minority thinks they should become violent and reject the will of the majority, because their views differ. In a rational society, it is the task of the minority to tell the people what they would do if they were the majority. If they do their job well and it is acceptable, then at election time they (minority) will become the majority.

***

It seems advisable during football practice to spend considerable time working under pressure and adversity, it is too late to do it during the game. The "pressure situations" include down, distance, and clock. "Adversity" is weather, field position, score, and injuries.

***

Assuming football ability, the ideal traits for a player would be the physical (the ability to keep his feet), the emotional: (to maintain composure under pressure), and the mental: (to know what is happening on the field).

***

Drills are an essential part of football technique development. It seems many drills are continued by tradition rather than need. Drills should be evaluated for their purpose. How do they fit into the fundamentals and techniques of the particular style of play of the team? After the "why?" comes the what. . . . Drills are divided into three general categories: conditioning, agility and technique. There may be a combination of these, but the football staff should know what role the drill plays.

***

The difference between the player who looks great in drills and the one who performs in the game is a matter of transfer. The largest gap in football performance is this inability to transfer techniques practiced in drills to techniques used on the playing field. The player and coach who can engineer this transfer will have a successful performance.

***

The game plan is incomplete if it includes only offensive and defensive patterns anticipated as being successful before the fact. The game plan needs to include three phases, first, the heart of the plan, what goes into the game to control the opponent; second, the "catch up" to be used when the team must gamble to get back into the game, and third, those situations where you need a single play for a chance to pull the game out.

***

Offensive satisfaction comes from proper execution and maintaining poise. Offense must maintain a controlled level of sustained intensity. The offense must avoid mistakes more than the defense. The objective is to score, that is the end result, but the control and discipline of offense requires a hold on the emotions. Aggressive, but calculated execution must be the highest order.

***

Defensive satisfaction comes from forcing the punt and preventing the score. Their objective is the disruption of the offensive attack; intimidating the offense with the hope of creating a loss of offensive poise. The defense must play with an explosive, reactive intensity. The defense must be disciplined and execute a plan; it reacts and in many ways must be more aggressive than the offense. The defense can compensate for individual breakdowns more readily than the offense.

***

Coaches always "talk" of emphasis on the kicking game, but few exercise this verbal commitment. The importance of the kicking game is obvious, but two things seem to negate the effort it requires. For the players there seems to be a mental block in the effort and discipline required. This is especially true of the punting effort and discipline required of the punting team. They often consider the need to punt as a result of failure. Thus, they approach it with a negative attitude. In reality it is the single biggest yardage per play the offense will have.

***

The second phase, to practice the kicking game, is disruptive to the practice routine and usually slower moving. This leads to impatience, leading to neglect. Also, within the kicking game there are so many variances to be worked on it seems there isn't time.

***

For both the player and coach, the kicking game is often treated as something that comes "after" offense or defense and there is a psychological let down in that phase of football.

***

Time is relentless, but it does have a past. Memories seem to diminish in time if they are associated with the negative allowing us to keep the good memories alive and vivid. The danger of the good memories, as time embellishes them, is it leads to people being regarded beyond their legitimate proportions.

***

It has been our experience that the only thing the "prevent defense" has done for us is to prevent us from saving the win. The reason may be that a change in alignments causes hesitant play. Possibly the very philosophy of the "prevent" causes the team to become too passive or it might be that it communicates a kind of "reverse panic." Through the years, more times than not, the opposition worked into scoring position when we were in the "prevent." Conversely, more times than not the opponent was denied scoring position in so called "prevent situations" when we played our normal defense.

***

The old adage in coaching about more teams being over-coached than under-coached isn't quite accurate. The enemy is time. Time dictates how much coaching can be done and to do too much for the time allotted will lead to a confused team. Football boils down to not what the coaches know, but to what the players can do.

***

A consideration in the philosophy of the "prevent defense" may be the exchange of personnel rather than a change of tactic. Certain personnel may be better able to execute in a "prevent" situation and can practice such a situation. The individual skills of the athlete should be a primary concern.

***

The role of manager isn't to restrict those he is managing, but to help them. The football coach, as a manager, should do all he can to assist those he is directing to be successful.

***

If a man has a responsibility then he must have the authority to exercise that responsibility. It is a management fault and a hindrance to morale to give a man an assignment if he is restricted in doing the things to back it up. To be successful in this, the man with responsibility cannot be irresponsible, he must be capable of doing the job within the format of the philosophy of the management concept.

***

Power is as it is perceived by others; only in confrontation is its validity tested.

***

Emphasis brings results.

***

The intellectual man is a pessimist, seeing pitfalls as a logical sequence. Spiritual man is an optimist, seeing only the goal to be reached. It is a good balance, for it is this balance that keeps the human being from self-destruction..

***

Evil may sustain itself because "good" feels guilty in fighting back.

***

Being a gifted athlete is a God-given talent. It is the obligation of the athlete to hone his talent and be the best he can be. A quality sometimes missing in the gifted athlete is "smart." Without being a smart athlete, the physical can work against him. As much as coaches want gifted athletes, they also want smart athletes. In the athletic situation there are times "smart" is better than "gifted." With proper preparation, the gifted can be smart though the opposite might not be true.

***

Those in charge may use rhetoric as a substitute for exercising their responsibilities and when the realities of the situation work against them they use criticism as a substitute for their failure.

***

Talent abounds. . . but it may go unnurtured or unnoticed if it isn't disciplined. The role of the coach and teacher is to recognize, discipline and nurture this talent.

***

In the pressures of recruiting, very important to success in recruiting an athlete is the athlete's ability to identify with the coach recruiting him not by being the "pal" of the athlete, but rather by the athlete sensing the coach is sincere, honest and truly interested in the athlete's welfare.

***

It has always intrigued me how, after reaching a certain age, you are considered too old for a job by people who are quite possibly older than you, and they themselves have a job. By their own rationale they should resign.

***

As Lou Brock has said, "You become old by edict. This age thing is a mystical ghost. It isn't what you can do. . . but what others think you can do."

***

If this "age barrier" was true, think of all the great world leaders who would have never led. How many were well advanced in years before they assumed power? Many were in their seventies. How many great inventions or benefits to mankind would have been lost by date of birth?

***

Health is more of a factor in having energy than is age. Enthusiasm, as well as curiosity is more a factor in having energy than is age.

***

Why does it seem so often, the just suffer injustice and the unjust seldom receive justice?

***

A cynic is most often nothing more than a frustrated idealist.

***

The injury to an organization is not the incompetent; rather it is the competent who have little faith in the competency of others.

***

On television, I heard an athlete responding to accolades for a great performance make the following reply, "Thank you. God favored me with talent, the performance only showed my appreciation."

***

The television series, "Roots," brought a great upswing in our national interest in genealogy--where we came from and who we came from? This is something no referee needs worry about. There is no football official whom a coach can't tell him where he came from. . . not only the past, but the coach can forecast the future. . . in telling him where he is going. The referee's origin and perversions are well known by most coaches.

***

The three great social issues of our time really have no change for two with only the individual able to change the third. The issues are:
Young versus old. . . hang on, the young will be old.
Race versus race. . .Skin isn't going to change.
Rich versus poor. . . This can go either way.
The moral is: The first is inevitable; the second unalterable and the third inconclusive.

***

The main problem in the "Generation Gap" is the old haven't given up their young ideas.

***

We often put labels on things. In human response to circumstances we call the champion of a cause oft times a militant. That is supposed to be a term of fear. We are all militants if we believe strongly in something. A militant is one who is active _for_ something. A hostile is the next step. For the hostile, emotion has interjected itself too strongly, but the hostile can be coped with. The belligerent is a threat. He may be unreasonable and provocative. He may have a penchant for violence. The one to fear is the fanatic. As the philosopher, Santayana said, "A fanatic is one who keeps fighting when the cause has been forgotten."

***

Bowl games are becoming like professional wrestling. A lot of show, but not much meaning. The polls name the top twenty teams in the country, but more than that are selected for bowl play.

***

If perceived power is real, then it is incumbent upon the holder of that power not to abuse it.

***

Assuming the data fed to a computer is accurate, the machine can draw conclusions, but only the human can make decisions. (Choices). Possibly the computer becomes an excuse for not making human decisions and thus would be the beginning of the evolution of machines truly running man.

***

Many athletes are superstitious in their approach to the game. They have those certain little quirks that they pay homage to before and during the contest. I have always thought such actions are unacknowledged prayers. Without associating it with a specific prayer, it is, in a way, the realization of a force beyond mortal man's understanding.

***

<u>The front page of the newspaper tells of human failure, the editorial page of dreams, and the sports page of accomplishments.</u>

***

If you don't like a person, don't make the mistake of underestimating him.

***

What is good about us in one circumstance is a negative in another. We all have the "defects of our virtues."

***

I remember when I was a boy, about the only advice my father gave me was, "two do's and two don'ts." The do's were: I could make a living anyway I wanted and I could marry whomever I wanted. The two don'ts: Don't fool around with somebody else's wife and don't fool around with somebody else's money.

***

In football, the fans often treat the coach as though he has violated the two don'ts. The team as their wife or mistress and the money made or lost as theirs. The financial pressure of major college athletics has forced many athletic departments to remain under the umbrella of education, but not to practice any philosophy or principles of education. The athletic program seems to be sliding farther and farther to a straight and pure business venture.

***

It is possible for the authorities to schedule financial success by playing too many games out of their level of competition for big gate receipts. (These games usually away from home). To do this, the business end of athletics may be in the black and for those people considered a winning season, but in the artistic sense, (winning) it is a failure. In this situation the artist (coach) is sacrificed to the business priority. Oh, Well! Few great artists have been appreciated in their own lifetime.

***

A true reality and possibly a tragedy is the basic conflict in which the coach may find himself. The institution sets the educational and deportment guidelines the program must operate under while the outside groups want only victories. If the former sets standards that won't allow the latter to have victories, then the coach is in the grinder because the simple truth is the guidesetters can't protect the coach from the scalp-hunters, though they, the guidesetters, have arranged the scalping. What is a coach to do?

***

Assuming some required athletic abilities, I believe the two most important physical needs of the football player are the ability to stay on his feet, followed quickly by the ability to move his feet. These two traits alone can make up for many shortcomings while the lack of them can neutralize many athletic strengths.

***

Some coaching staffs want to call all the plays from the sideline just so they know in advance what the call is and they can then observe opponent reactions. Though it would be late getting upstairs, I often wondered why the bench doesn't send a messenger out after every play. The messenger being the player coming out, bringing with him the play the QB called. There are times what is sent in and what is called aren't the same.

***

The coach is a throwback to the days of human sacrifice. He is the one sacrificed to the pagan gods (alumni and booster groups) to purge the sickness and cleanse and protect the masses.

***

The coach is often regarded as an entertainer or performer. Even if he is successful, after a time people want a change-- something to ogle and rejuvenate their curiosity. There have been winning coaches who were fired or on the precipice of oblivion. . . not because they lost, but they weren't winning "big enough" or they didn't pass enough or their family had pimples.

***

No one should enter the coaching profession without the love of a dog. Dog's love is pure. There are no "if's" as in the love among people. No conditions. Win or lose, when the coach goes home the dog is there, with his tail wagging. He doesn't know or care who played or what the score may have been.

***

One of the major things wrong with the coaching profession is the coaches themselves. Coaches are an aggressive, ambitious group and when one is professionally slain, there are hundreds anxious to take his place. The moral is: we are hired to be fired. After a few months, those hiring the coach are contemplating his replacement. In essence, the coach isn't respected by those who hire him. Discarding him is easy, expected, and often relished by others.

***

Americans often criticize America. This isn't a lack of loyalty, but rather the strength of our nation. With all our problems, it is interesting to note that in America, 4,000,000 farmers feed the nation and much of the world. In the Soviet Union 23,000,000 farmers can't feed Russia. To give an example, there are families in Russia with six members of the family having an income and they are unable to achieve American standards of living from one income.

***

The real scare isn't what is wrong with America, but our selfishness won't allow us to sacrifice when needed to keep us as we are. It is a symptom of collapse from within.

***

Truth, as related, isn't always truth. It is the truth from one point of view. It may be an honest presentation, but not always the pure truth.

***

The American court system doesn't promise a just trial or that justice will prevail. The effort is to try for justice. What the system promises is a "fair trial." That means as fair as the circumstances will allow. The same goes in coaching players. The coaching decisions may not always be "just" in regard to the players, but it should be fair.

***

It would be helpful to offensive football if, during practice, the offensive coaches would spend some time standing behind the defense to view offensive execution. It is an easier place to spot tip-offs than from standing behind the offense or watching films.

***

The defensive players and coaches should help the offense during practice by telling them of tip-offs and errors; and the offense should do the same for the defense. However, it is a noble motive not always done. Why? Because a player wants to look good for his coaches and anything helping him show better will be utilized. This is another hazard of platoon football and the almost separate nature of offensive and defensive football.

***

In regard to the academic faculty's understanding of the athletic pressures and realities, it seems, as a generalization, those in science and math have a more realistic understanding than those from the humanities. It could be because one group views athletics with factual realism while the second group is more utopian.

***

The coach must be careful not to confuse the athletic ability with the individual. An athlete may be a very poor performer and out of his element at the level of competition and the coach, evaluating the player as a "poor one," may tend to let this feeling spill over into his judgment of the individual as a human being. As there are fine athletes who are "bad" people, there are also poor athletes who are super people. The coach must keep the evaluation between performer and performance separated.

***

Television and the dollars it generates have brought professional sports stars unbelievable financial reward. So much so, it has alienated the fan from the athlete. He is regarded as an entertainer and performer . . .and he had better not have any bad performances. The athlete is often apart from his home team fans and, through this alienation, loyalties are diminished.

***

How much of a salary cut would Michael Jordan or Dan Marino take if they became President of the United States. Today many pro athletes earn a $1,000,000 per year.. One earning $1,000,000.00 per year, is being paid about $115.00 per hour, day and night, twenty-four hours a day, twelve months a year.

***

How much money is a lot of money? How much is a billion dollars? What would be a yardstick of comparison? If you spent $1000 a day, every single day from the day of the crucifixion until 1987 you would spend a billion dollars. Or, it was just a little over one billion minutes ago Christ was walking the earth.

***

It seems many fanatic or semi-fanatic hate groups are headed by a deranged leader while many joining the cause, join not from conviction or lofty purpose, but rather as a way of getting something they want. . .Attention.

***

Personal success and honors are fleeting and soon forgotten and become reminiscenes of those they have passed by. In coaching, the lasting contentment comes from knowing those playing for you are living their lives well and you had a part in it.

***

Turning the "other cheek" may have a value in the hereafter, but while in this life you just take a beating. . . be you an individual or a nation.

***

The coaching profession may be the ultimate example of the free enterprise system. You not only plan, work and pray for your success, but you hope all others fail.

***

Dropping a player from a team for disciplinary reasons may be the only solution for the welfare of the group, but it should be a last resort. Dropping the player may be avoiding and ignoring a problem. . . it is the easy way out. The athletic "tool" may be the only avenue of assisting the youngster. Take that away and you lose the only lever available.

***

The 1980 Super Bowl, Pittsburgh versus Los Angeles, the cost for a sixty second commercial on television was $480,000.00... and they call it a game. There is good and bad in this and some of the "bad" filters into the colleges and the high schools, in 1999 the price was $1,500,000 per thirty seconds.

***

Coaches, for the most part, are "liberal-conservatives." It is a difficult paradox to define. On most social issues, where human rights and dignity are involved, coaches are most liberal and progressive. The very actions of the coaches on social issues have been almost in anticipation, or initial action of functional support. Yet, any challenge to the coach's regimen and authority is ruggedly opposed. On matters of the coach-player relationship the coach is very conservative.

***

If one studies art, music or dance in college the person is considered a sensitive, aesthetic person; but if one studies physical education, then the person is considered to be less than bright and pursuing a somewhat primeval endeavor. Physical education and athletics are certainly an expressive art form. In fact, art, music, dance, athletics and physical education have more in common than not. Just as most of man's religions have more similarity than not. . . so do the various aesthetics.

***

Success and failure become near conditioned responses. This takes place because of reinforcement. Success or failure is always "because of . . ." with the result soon one believes. Certain teams wait to lose while others know they will win. In victory one strives in anticipation; in defeat, one expects and accepts the outcome.

***

The power of the mind in football is never ignored, but really not understood. In athletics it is often heard one has gained their "second wind." Physiology says there is no such thing. There are psychologists who insist what is known as "second wind" is really a form of self-hypnosis, with the brain (mind) taking control of the physiological stress.

***

Reaction to losing is emotional, especially for the public who clamor for the scalp of a losing coach. Logic will not be considered. Seldom has logic controlled emotion; if it did there would be far fewer "crimes of passion." When the public comes after a coach it is truly 'mob action' in many cases. Logic is discarded; emotion takes hold and the effect snowballs. The lesson: You better know your situation is one with an equal chance of success against the competition.

***

Athletics in its purest sense has been a value beyond the book; now academics through technology, is teaching beyond the book. Television, cassettes, etc., are teaching without the printed word. Nothing replaces the printed word in learning how to think. Learning aids and resources should <u>assist</u>, not <u>replace</u> the printed word.

***

A fact not faced is of itself anti-intellectual. Authority placed in the hands of anti-intellectuals lead to a repressive society.

***

In coaching or anything else for that matter, teaching is secondary to learning. If one isn't willing to learn, then teaching can't take place. In coaching, it is important that the players be willing to learn.

***

The pressure of winning is more oppressive than that of losing. In losing all look for self-absolvements and scapegoats. In winning, each feels he is a part of it. This pressure from winning drives the performer to win again. The team regards each opponent as a challenge: "Is this the team that is going to beat us?" This serves as a motivation for further success. It is rooted in apprehension.

***

Losing erodes attitude and concentration; winning erodes excitement.

***

A repressive society must attempt to implant and systemize ignorance. Ignorance is essential for perpetuation of repression. However, ignorance and repression may dull thinking, but the mind of man won't and can't stay shackled.

***

Football is a strange game. It is the only sport that is two separate games in one. With the present rules, platoon football, the offense and defense play almost independently of each other. Each has their own coaches; meetings and game plans. This leads to internal rivalries and hostilities within a team that can tear it apart. Be on guard, coaches must prevent a complete isolation of offense from defense. If not, all they will have in common is uniform and game time.

***

College football, as have people and institutions, has been corrupted by money. Not for the money itself, but for the need to have it to maintain the program. There are some colleges where the college administration has "sold out" to outside interests.

***

Proponents of football need to speak and act in a manner that is beneficial to the game. As I once read somewhere, "neutralism is nationalism with an inferiority complex." The game is big, popular and a part of our culture. It is easy for it to stray. If the football coaching profession doesn't take care of its own house, then those with little sympathy or understanding will put the house in order for them.

***

Thinking about football and its mystique leads to thinking about other things. About the human spirit and the drive to excel. . . the intangibles that make man do more than just exist. I think of the sea as nature's laboratory for creation and the mountains as its church spires. . .and between the two man and beast roam in search of what they will never know.

***

Deeply committed and involved athletic participation is a spiritual experience. Maybe even mystical. Regardless of the structure of the game, it is a creative experience.

***

Charity is one's love for mankind, while loyalty is one's love for a friend.

***

Athletics is an art form, pure and simple. The athlete is the performer and the audience is the participant. To watch an athletic event is no different than to watch a play or a symphony.

***

There are some similarities, but one great difference between athletic competition and selling a service or product... selling is "comparative competition," while athletics is "combative competition."

***

<u>The only power without responsibility is God, closely followed by the press.</u>

***

A cliché may well be a fact proved valid by time.

***

Change, in itself, may not be progress, but a commitment to change may be.

***

Change must have direction and channel. As with progress, change can be meaningless, regressive, or repressive.

***

Philosophy is the "why." Strategy is "how." Tactic is "what."

***

I read someplace the great artists of our time aren't musicians, artists, etc., rather the great artists of our time are the accountants.

***

In testing that has been done, participants in individual sports have more personal traits of independence and self-reliance than does the "team sport" participant. However, the "team athlete" shows to be better in cooperation, interdependence and working toward a common goal.

***

In records we kept, individual participants, (those from tennis, wrestling, track, etc.) achieved higher grades in college than team participants. Within the football team, over a number of years, the average grade point average went as follows: Highest GPA offensive linemen followed by the linebackers. It seemed the more natural athletic talent utilized, the lower the GPA.

***

A good team means a number of things to those who follow it. There are sociological and psychological benefits, but reduced to its simplest element, it just allows people to gather and cheer for something. . . spontaneous and on the spot. "Fan Fun!"

***

As humans move through life, including coaches and players, there are repetitive phases. The creative phase, the routine phase and the rejuvenation phase. It plays a part in the approach and sustaining of the coaching situation.

***

A football staff should attempt to be a total staff--totality, in its personality. No single person can be all to all people, but a football staff, with numbers, can manage to have personal traits among the coaches to comprise a complete personality, somebody to appeal to each player.

***

The head football coach should provide the staff of assistants with the three "R's:" respect, responsibility and recognition.

***

Often members of the academic community see the football situation as one where the athletes are intellectual inferiors who are willingly exploited and have no interest beyond football. The coaches are perceived as sinister, devious, deceitful exploiters and users of the athletes who are not as bright as academics and are not in the academic mainstream. The coaches are not to be trusted. The academic community believes they know more about athletics than those who are living it and only the faculty is capable of making intelligent judgments regarding athletics. None of the above are axioms and far more untrue than true.

***

Outsiders often make generalizations based on isolated instances.

***

John Adams once said, "Democracy commits suicide." It seems athletics may suffer the same disorder.

***

The shame of national cynicism is that it leads to the erosion of patriotism. Erosion of patriotism to the national spirit is akin to erosion of hope to the human spirit. If only in a limited atmosphere for a minimum of time, football can rekindle a kind of patriotism.

***

Defensive football must be played with a coherent frenzy.

***

The over-riding value of athletic participation is two-fold. First, it allows one to know self under stress and secondly, it develops a respect for others--both teammates and opponents. These two qualities are possibly the most important in going through life.

***

The three major wastes of coaches and players are the three "P's:" potential, prejudice and procrastination.

****

Champions thrive on challenge. Challenge lights the fire in some and is an extinguisher to others. Champion isn't synonymous with victory, it is the trait of the individual.

***

It may be the only choice, with no alternatives, but the athlete living off-campus is at a great disadvantage in many ways. He is isolated from student activities on campus. He is more readily able to miss classes and above all, the lifestyle usually leads to inferior eating habits.

***

We have allowed our senior football players to move off campus the last semester of their senior year. This has worked out well for a number of reasons. It lets them get out of what regimentation there is in the dorm; they can get experience in living on their own (shopping, cooking, cleaning, etc.), and obviously they have a freedom of life-style unavailable in any dorm or fraternity situation.

***

By the time they reach this stage of their college careers, they have demonstrated that they are academically responsible and can demonstrate the maturity it takes to be responsible. Selfishly from the football standpoint, it allows room for any mid-semester entries to the program and removes those players who have no more responsibility to the football program.

***

Our experience has been just about the same, the footballers are anxious to move off campus, but after about a month or so, the dorm seems pretty good to them. Off campus "corn flakes" for dinner seems almost routine.

***

One of the nice things about the athletic dorm was having group study sessions. A number of players taking the same class during study hours would study as a group; asking each other questions and discussing what was not easily understood. I have no doubt these peer meetings helped in academic success.

***

Maybe there should be consideration given to eliminating any special group dorms. How about the foreign language school dorm or the music dorm or the business students, or science students . . . international students, etc.? The athletic dorm, academically, isn't as specialized as many of the academic or ethnic dorms that are considered compatible with education.

***

As a generalization the major football powers are fairly well defined by the "have's" and the "have-not's." Now and then a maverick makes a temporary incursion into the elite group, but over-all it remains the same. Some are on the short end of the stick because of money, admissions, curriculum, philosophy, etc., as the nature of the institution makes it difficult to sustain a program. However, there are others who never gain the level of success they strive for though they have the same advantages as the rabbit they are chasing. A tradition of success may be the missing ingredient.

***

Some of the "have-not's" must play year in and year out against the prestige football schools. This means they must compete with the traditionally successful programs for the same players. Yet the have-nots are at a great disadvantage to attract the athletes in sufficient numbers. Because of this they often enroll the young man who is a quality football player, but may not be the quality person their competition attracts. It may well be that this "character" difference is the reason the big winners didn't recruit the youngster.

***

If not careful, the end result will be that the "have-not's" may have some fine football players, but they bring into the program poor attitudes and morale and possible academic and social problems.

***

The good program, whether they realize it or not, must recruit the youngster with the assumption he will be with the program for four years to make his full contribution. Players who don't last their entire term are the exception rather than the rule and an investment loss to the college.

***

The quickest and easiest way to solve a problem is to eliminate it. I am not sure that is a solution to the problem, but it is a solution to the situation. It is resolved, not solved.

***

I have always believed dropping a player from the team and from scholarship is a last resort. The primary question must be, what effect does this have on the young man? Will he have to forfeit his education? Without opportunity or resources to pursue it elsewhere? Is he at the stage in life where it is important he learn he must be responsible for his acts with subsequent consequence? Young enough where a good "swift kick in the pants" is needed, but he can recover, having learned and goes on? What effect will it have on the remainder of the team and program?

***

Players are surprisingly patient and intuitive with their teammates. They sense when a player needs to be straightened out within the program and when he should be eliminated. Over the years, almost every player I have dropped from a team has later said that he deserved it and that it was the best thing that happened to him. All of a sudden something serious was the consequence for his lack of responsibility.

***

If it is decided there is no way we can keep the young man on the team, but without the scholarship he would forfeit his chance of ever getting an education, then I have kept him on aid, but divorced him from the program.

***

Anytime I have dropped a player from the team I truly feel I have failed.

***

Something John Ralston said to me at a low point in my career, has stayed with me ever since. "Success and failure are measures of materialistic things. . .including public acclaim." They seem worldly measures, yet as he felt at one time, and as I did at that stage of my career, by public acclaim and treatment we would be registered as failures. We didn't win enough games or the "big" game some fool determined as earth-shaking. Yet, at this time, thought to have failed in the public's eye, we both felt very successful given the situation we had to work in. I thought to myself, "It is as though I have failed, yet I know I was very successful and another would reap the rewards of what I had begun." That hurts!

***

That should be the measure. <u>If you fulfill your responsibilities to family, occupation, integrity, etc., and you are fulfilled in what you are doing, then that is really success. To fulfill your responsibilities, but feel empty, non-contributing and a "quiet despair" about what you are doing, then how can you be "successful?" To satisfy the material things in life, but to be empty in spirit in what you are doing, must be failure.</u>

***

In the late sixties, there was the realization that athletics was a vehicle for political statement by the black athlete and a polarization took place. There was little interaction and often hostility between the black and white athletes.

***

Then it turned where the white athletes tried to imitate the black athlete in dress, style, language and communication. Besides being "fun" for the white athlete, in a way, it was a way of communicating to the black athlete that we are all one.

***

In the present cycle, each answers to his own drummer with a much more respectful, acceptable communication among all. It is one of mutual respect and understanding. Certainly an indication that the family of man can live together. However, it seems there are tensions emerging that may see this evaporate.

***

There are many pros and cons in having an athletic dorm. I understand those who are opposed on philosophical grounds. In practical matters it is a great boost. Not in terms of having a 'military atmosphere,' but the channeling of common endeavors and problems. From the academic standpoint it has worked out well. The athletes have the same time problem between their athletic and academic commitment. It helps to establish a compatible routine. In a situation where they (athletes) are spread all over the campus, we have found the study and social habits of the general student body create problems for the athletes.

***

There is concern the athletic dorm isolates the athletes from the student-body. I haven't found this to be true. If there is a partial truth to it, what is the difference between an athlete living with others with a common interest than living in a fraternity house with the same goal?

***

From a strictly selfish, football viewpoint, the athletic dorm may be one of the only places a good "team feeling" may be developed. Football is the only game where offense and defense function as nearly two separate entities. It is organized this way: the athletic dorm may be one of the few places where interaction among the defense and offense takes place.

***

All in all, as in any human situation, there are advantages and disadvantages. My feeling is that the athletic dorm provides more positives than the opposite. Social, academic, athletic, living habits, etc., are all better supervised.

***

Four of the seven colleges where I was head coach we had a football dorm. As any such dorm we had the pranksters. Childish stuff. Fire extinguishers expended; water fights in the hall. . . the interesting point, at no time were any players of color involved. Some thought the pranks were a product of "honkey" immaturity; others said the dorm was as nice a place as they had ever lived and wouldn't mess it up.

***

The dorms were at schools in Pennsylvania, Utah, North Carolina and Oregon, covering a time span of over twenty-five years and not one "Halloween" type prank in the dorms from the minority segment of our population . . . brown, black or Asian.

***

Aristotle was the only western philosopher to believe luck or chance play a part in life.

***

The three virtues are: temperance, courage and justice. The first two are for self, the third for others. The words belief and proof are incompatible. One is a fact. . .the other a conviction that may be a fact.

***

Beauty is the highest form of pleasure.

***

The four states of life according to Aristotle are: 1. Rest (sleep) 2. Play (complete unto itself) 3. Toil (means of subsistence) 4. Leisure (time of thought).

***

Leisure is the opposite of play; leisure is very demanding.

***

Applied sciences produce; philosophy directs.

***

One can be disloyal without uttering a word. There is the disloyalty of silence. There are times silence can be as disloyal as any words spoken. Times where silence is interpreted as support, rather than the words, to refute the allegation or assumption.

***

Human suffering hurts me deeply and haunts me. Yet it makes me thankful for what I have and sometimes feel guilty for having it.

***

Human compassion humbles me and brings tears. It makes me feel the "God" in man.

***

The human spirit is my closest and most awesome communication with my Creator. It is thrilling, an act of faith and inspiration.

***

Peter Drucker, a world famous consultant to business on organization states that the discharge of responsibilities isn't good or bad as far as the person is concerned, rather a matter of right and wrong. A good man may be doing a bad job because he is wrong for it.

***

In a way, time out of coaching is excellent. It can allow one to evaluate, consider, etc., in the broadest terms of the game and human relations. . . not just in regard to "my team" and the opposition. From this time of evaluation and meditation, a better coach than before will emerge.

***

As Aristotle said, "creativity is a product of leisure." When active in coaching much of what we do is a matter of toil, but leisure is the time of regeneration and creative thoughts.

***

As a coach I would like to have been regarded as among the best in my profession. However, if the price for this is having only a few players graduate and a few players make the pros, while the majority of the players in our program aren't any better off than if they hadn't participated at all, my conscience would shriek. I would then be little more than a "slave trader." This I could not tolerate. I must feel we have served <u>all</u> those in our program the very best we can.

***

It well may be that the strongest "hates" in the world are based on the most passionate loves. One who loves country without question can then hate another nation because of that blind love. Religious wars would be a great example of such a love-hate relationship.

***

Arnold Toynbee, in speaking of nations, could just as well have been speaking of individuals when he stated that to the nation it is challenge and response. Does one surrender or respond to the challenge? In human life, do we surrender or respond to personal misfortune?

***

While at Utah State, Indiana University of Pennsylvania, and U.S. Coast Guard Academy, we were good in pressure situations. If we had a scoring opportunity we usually took advantage of it. If we had a sudden turnover in our favor we took advantage of it. Yet, at Wake Forest we had the same situations without the same results. I thought it was a lack of confidence; then a lack of mental toughness; then a lack of conditioning or a combination of these factors.

***

Mental toughness and conditioning really didn't seem factors because we had prepared the same way in both the good and bad situations. The "confidence" factor remained real, but is somewhat intangible. I have come to the conclusion that the difference was a matter of concentration. We may think of it as a lack of confidence, but it is more like excitement. A team that hasn't had great success, when faced with an opportunity, gets excited and loses its concentration. What must be developed is "concentration and control of excitement under pressure." It is important not to eliminate excitement, but to channel and use it. Excited concentration is the aim.

***

True, the good Lord has given us varying degrees of intelligence. Heredity would be the source of not bright to very bright and all the points in between. Environment may have an influence on ignorance versus knowledge, but ignorance and knowledge aren't synonymous with intelligence.

***

If we are normal, then none know everything and none know nothing. Ignorance, in itself, is curable. It may take interest, etc., but it can be corrected. What is sad is the rejection of knowledge and the choice to remain ignorant.

***

We in coaching can do much to encourage those in our care to take up the advantages education offers. Not just text book learning or becoming a "fact fool," rather it is living, exchanging and having interaction with others that creates and provides an education and knowledge in itself.

***

To be ignorant is sad, but to remain ignorant by one's own choice or lack of confidence is a crime.

***

I'm a "dog lover." I sometimes wonder why humans can become so attached to dogs. Sometimes it seems they get more affection from man than man is willing to give another human being. I think the reason for this is a mutual bond, or "love" without strings; the dog doesn't give devotion with strings attached. He isn't a friend, with an "if" attached. Sometimes in our human relations there is a string. . ."I'll be your friend" or "I'll love you if.. . ".or "I love you because. . ." with always a selfish motive involved somewhere. With the dog, you can give to each other and it is pure; there are no strings attached.

***

The dog is a good friend. Good times or bad, he'll be a friend. All he wants in return is to be treated as a friend.

***

We often go through life seeking happiness. That is the wrong word. . .we should be seeking a rewarding and interesting life. Happy changes from day to day or even minute to minute, but being comfortable is a more reasonable goal and a more consistent state of being.

***

It has always intrigued me, when an athlete or group of athletes complain to the athletic director about a program, the malcontents are taken as gospel, but those who think the program is in good order are ignored or never sought out. Actually, if the superior wants to "shoot the coach down," the malcontent becomes his ally; and the pro-program athletes are ignored.

***

In essence, it means the tools at hand are used, depending upon the disposition of the superior.

***

Unity in any group endeavor is vital, but not at the expense of individuality. If individuality is subverted rather than directed, it can cause downfall. Without individuality, there is no adjustment to crisis or no replacement for the leader of the unit. The unit becomes a martinet. Tunnel vision and utter collapse result if the leader symbol is removed. The job in a team sport is to direct the individuals to work together for a common goal. . .not blind allegiance in itself.

***

Job descriptions proclaim perfection; but the description is performed by imperfect people.

***

Football or anything else, winning breeds winning and losing breeds losing. A winning team believes it is going to win. They feel and know something is going to happen to make them win. . .the losing team waits to lose. They stand back and watch themselves become defeated.

***

In 1971, in the final game of the season against Ray Guy and his Southern Mississippi University team, we were tied with a few seconds left in the game. Guy stood in the end zone to punt and preserve the tie. Our defensive end rushed in, blocked the punt and recovered it for a touchdown. It was the only punt Guy ever had blocked in college. After the game the player, who blocked the punt, said, "I knew we would win!" He won it but my concern was he sure waited a long time to win it. Cutting it that close did me little good for the previous fifty-nine and three quarter minutes.

***

There is more hope than control in this thought. Heavenly hope, that you will work for strong, honest people who have the courage to stand up to adversity. I have worked for some who lacked courage. . . not the physical kind that is a result of losing their temper. . .but the kind that is ignoble. Those who quiver or cower under any kind of pressure and, whatever pressure is on them, pass it on to you. You are their escape.

***

That doesn't mean always they are agreeable, or that they are right, or that you follow blindly. No! They are allowed human failings, as we all have, but you hope you have superiors who have a basic morality and integrity and who try (note the word try, they may not be 100% at it) to act in a decent moral manner.

***

Remember, when the sycophants and moral cowards we associate with reach decisions applied by pressures and fear, aren't going to admit to it. They will philosophize and rationalize. . . but seldom verbalize the "truths."

***

Don't be misled. I have been. In many coaching situations the educators espouse all the trite dialogue we are used to in our profession, i.e., the place of athletics, what it should be, and where it fits at that particular school. You may be doing just what they want when you operate your football program exactly as they describe. They may support you verbally and truly believe they are backing you. Often the faculty (or its agents), establish the rules and guidelines for the program, curriculum, admissions, etc. In the end, when the money people want a change, no matter how well you tried to operate your program within the university's professed policies, these same faculty people who establish the ground rules and with whom you have cooperated, can't or won't save you from the "wolves" on the prowl.

***

There are people, who by society's standards, are very successful, reaching their goals by unjustly destroying others. Even unsuccessful folks have done the same. The vanquished rationalize the villains "will get theirs!" That is based on a leap of faith that life is just and good. Based on observation and personal experience. . .there had better be a Hereafter. . . because, it seems, they aren't going to "get theirs" this time around.

***

It has been said that justice has been kidnapped by legal proceedings and is being held hostage in a law book somewhere.

***

I do believe good and evil exist. I don't know if they are separate, independent forces or just a trait of nature. A vacuum exists between the two and evil fills the vacuum. <u>By its very nature, good is slow to react to evil. Good will not accept evil as a force just because good is good. By the time good realizes what evil is doing it is often too late. When good decides to fight back, then a convulsion results because evil has gained such a strong foothold. Evil had captured the vacuum.</u>

***

The appeasement of Hitler prior to WW II is an example. He could have been stopped early. But in his early aggressions, "good" thought he could be reasoned with and permitted the aggressions to stand. When good decided it was dealing with evil and had to defend itself. . . a catastrophe resulted.

***

That alone is the primary dilemma in which most coaches are placed. This is the dilemma that leads to most of the problems in athletics: educational and institutional philosophy (jargon) versus the money people. One group of well meaning idealists can cripple you; the second group are often unreasonable realists who eliminate you.

***

Discipline is another word for organization. It allows diverse personalities and needs to meet on mutual ground. Discipline isn't a "dirty word." It means putting things in order and working in a cooperative manner towards a goal.

***

Seldom can discipline be imposed. It must be accepted. To impose it requires a police state or a fascist type order. To have a disciplined team, family or business, the people involved must accept it. I never had a disciplined team by imposing rules. Imposing discipline just means clandestine circumvention.

***

I have changed our team rules and discipline to the word "guidelines." Not to soften the meaning of the word, but an actual meaning to the word. A rule must never be broken, but that is a difficult situation, demanding a kind of perfection from an imperfect human being. "Guideline" is to be adhered to, but they allow a certain latitude to encompass particular situations.

***

Fear of failure can motivate winning teams.

***

Failure to try because of fear--is guaranteed failure.

***

Losing is not death; it just means we didn't achieve in the latest effort though we can achieve again tomorrow. Death is final; losing is not--it is transitional.

***

People must seek ways to express the earthly manifestation of soul, which is the human spirit; it may be direct or vicarious. Sports are a way to express this spirit.

***

So many limits on human performance and human spirit are self-imposed. For example the bumble bee, according to all principles of aerodynamics, can't fly.

***

In just about every sport, team or individual, it often seems the outstanding performers rise to conquer an opponent when defeat seems to be peering at them. How often will a championship team be losing a game for fifty-eight minutes and win in the last two and just the opposite, how many times the losing team (traditionally) will be winning for the same minutes and lose in the last moments of the game? The difference must be the confidence of one striving to win and the other waiting to lose. It must be in the mind and not the body. In five years at Wake Forest, we lost five games with seconds left. As the team improved, we reached the point where we had chances to grasp victory in the last seconds three times. We didn't accomplish it, but we had gained enough confidence and poise where we were attacking for victory at the end.

***

Ethnic neighborhoods, by race, religion, or economics (disadvantaged) encourage the gifted of the community to push onward and do better. Be it educationally or in athletics, arts, etc., they are encouraged to "beat the system" they are in. After they achieve success or the goal they have been encouraged to pursue, it seems they are often alienated or ostracized from the very ones who have encouraged them; the rationale being that individual is "no longer one of us!" So, at the same time he is encouraged and respected he is laying the groundwork for hostility and alienation.

***

It seems in many ways, the American stature is eroded. If we desert our friends our global enemies feel we have lost our will. This moral surrender leads adversaries to seek material gains. At home corruption within government and big business seem rampant.

***

Mao-tse-tung wrote in his essay <u>Contradictions,</u> "The people should make any alliance to defeat its greatest enemy." This would make any alliance acceptable to achieve this end. If thought about, that is a terrifying but realistic thought. Examples: Nationalist and Communist Chinese band together to defeat the Japanese before turning on each other; or Hitler at a loss as to why the USA wasn't his ally against communist Russia.

***

This may be an acceptable reality if not an ethical one and, in many ways, is an explanation of the devious and unethical conduct sometime a part of athletics.

***

Not all differences and convictions are right versus wrong nor good versus bad. Both views can be right but different from one's perspective. Different points of view can both be right or both wrong; at times it is good versus bad or right versus wrong, but it isn't axiomatic.

***

After a year as an assistant with the Chiefs I spent four subsequent summers when the rookies came in. This was in the late 60's and early 70's. It was my observation that there was a larger gulf between the northern black players and the southern black players than there was between black and white. The northern players regarded themselves as more aggressive, better educated and more sophisticated. The irony of all of this...black organized crime, I have been told by a most reliable source, is organized and operated by southerners... with the northerners working for them.

***

We often ascribe failure to the negative outcome of another's effort. We say they have failed...but have they? The only source who truly knows if the failure is a failure is the one who others say has failed. Often, though negative, for the individual it may be a success.

***

It is not unusual for a youngster to be pressured into attending a school other than the kid's preference. This is sometimes solved by flunking out of school. This may be regarded by others as a failure. Not for the youngster. It may be regarded by that individual as a success. Though the hard way, the youngster got away from where there was no desire to be.

***

It wasn't unusual for a youngster coming into our football program from high school or junior college who had a reputation of being hard to handle, or always getting into fights or always acting the clown. More often than not, when such kids joined our program they conducted themselves just the opposite. Youngsters in grade school and high school are often cast in certain roles and they feel it is important to play that role to retain their identity. A new school, a new environment and new friends lets a different person emerge. They have outgrown the past image and the new environment let's it be shed.

***

We recruited a junior college linebacker one time. . .and he was a good one. His reputation was that in every high school and junior college game he played in he got in a fight. Our instruction to him. . . the first fight and he was gone. He was relieved at this edict; he started every game he played for us; was a hellacious football player. . . and not close to a fight. He became what he wanted to be not what the hometown image said he was.

***

Two words make up the most beautiful and the ugliest in our range of emotions. Compassion is beautiful, beyond love; it isn't sympathy, it isn't selfish, it has no strings. It is the caring for others without self-serving motives. We tell our players the ugliest word and the biggest waste of time is prejudice. Prejudice, not with reason based on experience and fact, but the prejudice that is the opposite of compassion. A prejudice not based on valid reason, is selfish and self-defeating. How many great experiences, human and otherwise, we have all missed because of unfounded prejudices? There is a difference between discrimination and discriminating. You can have the latter without the former.

***

Somewhere in the past I heard the following and it has always stuck with me. . .
"He who knows not and knows not he knows not. . .is a fool, avoid him. He who knows not and knows he knows not. . .is dumb, teach him. He who knows and knows not he knows,. . .is asleep, awake him. He who knows and knows he knows. . .is a wise man, follow him."

***

Having knowledge isn't wisdom; "wisdom" is the facility to use knowledge.

***

Though the defense still must react to the offense, in modern defensive play there is just as much emphasis on the offense reacting to the dictates of the defense. Many defensive adjustments are made before the snap of the ball while many of the offensive adjustments are made after the snap of the ball. Defense may be an improper term, though true, it is being attacked and must defend itself; but in many ways defense is played more like the offense, but without the ball.

***

It was once said that a cliché was, "A truth proved valid by time." A cliché that always struck me funny was the prophetic one heard so often, "All things being equal (x) would make the difference". Really, it is saying that if everything else is equal, but one thing, then the team with that single superiority will win. Consequently then, all things aren't equal. Better said, if all things are equal, but one thing, then that one would be the difference.

***

Champions cope with challenge. A team in a championship game for the first time often fail. They haven't faced that challenge before. The challenge to the champion serves as a boost and a drive to succeed. To the newcomer, challenging to be the champion becomes an inhibiting factor. This is overcome by experience and exercising the confidence that brought the team as far as it has.

***

Winning streaks are far more pressure filled than losing streaks. Losing, everybody has a reason; everybody wants out; everybody blames the next guy; but in winning, each player doesn't want to be the one to cause defeat. The frame of mind becomes one that motivates the team for each game because of the constant fear that each team played is the one who may defeat them.

***

If a team gives 110 percent it will win. Or a player is a "110 percenter," but that seems incongruent with the facts. If 100 percent is the ultimate, then 110 percent is impossible. It doesn't exist. In essence we are striving for performance matching or trying to match potential. The team that performs closer to their potential (100 percent) is the optimum we strive for. Now, individuals may have more potential than they realize. . . but the goal isn't 110 percent.

***

It may have a "George Orwell" ring to it, but one of the things we have attempted to do, with some success, is to assign an upperclassman to a frosh in the pre-season and first semester of college--just to know how he is doing and look after him on occasion.

***

This has helped us to overcome the division between varsity and frosh and allows the frosh to know an upperclassman who is approachable to him. The upperclassman can sense frustration, discouragement and homesickness and if the "big brother" can't head it off, at least he can get word to the coaches.

***

By doing this, our freshman attrition dropped way down. This isn't a constant companion situation, it is eating with him at a meal now and then, sticking your head in his room, and walking with him to some team function. It has been a great help in combating freshmen withdrawal symptoms.

***

This system has given us an honest check on social habits, academic welfare, and football concerns of the new men trying to adjust to a new life-style. It has been helpful to the staff.

***

Many courses of action are determined by pettiness and vindictiveness, but as a rationalization, philosophical reasons espouse. It is much the same with wars. So many wars, fought for economical or despot reasons are done in the "name of God."

***

Great minds discuss ideas, good minds discuss events, and small minds discuss people.

***

Experience is a teacher only if you have learned something.

***

Too often education, indoctrinates and institutionalizes rather than liberates.
Much of education creates a problem for which it has a solution; problems without solutions are avoided.

***

The foolishness of it all.......
Charlie McClendon (L.S.U.) and Bill Battle (Tennessee,) both were fired in the Southeast conference by schools with a winning record of over 70 percent.

***

Claude Gilbert was 8-3 in 1979 and 57-18 overall at San Diego State. That is a winning percentage close to 76 percent. In 1980 he was 4-8 and fired.

***

The public address announcer at T.C.U. announced S.M.U. had upset Texas. At the time T.C.U. was losing to Baylor 6-7. The P.A. announcer was fired after the game, the logic being his announcement spurred Baylor to a 21-6 win. A Texas loss gave Baylor the SWC championship. (T.C.U. was 1-10 on the season and Baylor 10-1).

***

Respect your opponent for the work and effort he has put into his play. He has earned it; see to it you have earned his respect by your play. If you and each teammate is successful in your individual effort, then the team will be a success.

***

Everybody is somebody; find out who that somebody is. . . find out who you are, then you will know what you can do.

***

It is intriguing, when an athletic program is punished for violating the rules. Media columnists disseminate a profusion of columns on the sanctity and purity needed in athletics. They insist it is but a game, etc., yet many of these same writers will assist in creating the pressures that lead to violations.

***

Do not be deceived by education. . .or rather, by what education is. Many who believe they are educated deceive themselves. Many people are holders of numerous and impressive degrees. . .yet does that ensure education or rather signify training and specialization? Bigotry, prejudice by emotion and not by reason can be traits of the trained, but shouldn't be of the educated.

***

College can expand your horizons and give you some training, but if most of all you have "learned how to learn." you have accomplished much. If you know your own worth and have self-mastery, know your _real_ you, are tolerant of others and respect other's interests, dreams and motivation, knowing they are important to them if not to you. . .then you are educated. My experience, regardless of age, has been that I have run into far more people who are trained than educated.

***

I am taking from Sam Levenson, but it is so true and in such danger as our society becomes more computerized and isolated from "people encounters." He said the five senses of speech, hearing, taste, smell and touch are the five senses that make up consciousness. The sixth sense, love, empathy, compassion. . .that is conscience.

***

Billy Martin, who, at various times in his life was manager of the New York Yankees, was a most interesting man. The situation is worth thinking about . In spite of constant public airing of his problems with players and management, the fans supported him in a most active way. Why?

***

In my opinion he bridged the gap between fan and team. With athletes being paid more money in a season or two than most will make in a lifetime; wanting to switch from one team to another at their discretion; alienating the fans and communicating no loyalty to town or team, Martin became a symbol. He stood up to the highly paid super-star. He represented the feeling of the average fan toward the individual player.

***

Billy Martin represented "Joe Fan" sentiments in their hostility and disillusionment toward the player who travels the personal road only.

***

Intellect void of morality may be the most dangerous threat to mankind.

***

The way things are going, we will soon be back to pioneer days in America. People will grow their own food, make their own clothes and ride bikes for transportation. They will barter for goods. It seems the only way to meet head-on the high cost of living in our technological society.

***

It seems "fending" for ourselves is the only way to assert and protect ourselves from the fear, real or not, that . big business is cheating us. That we are really being cheated of the basic principles of America. Cars are recalled by the tens of thousands and there is the general aura of mistrust that has been created in government and industry. It appears the great growth industry of our nation is "ripping" people off. Public officials, and big business, all take their toll on the public confidence. It seems the robber with a gun in his hand is an honest crook. You know, right up front, what he wants. He steals my material things, but when government officials and large industries rob, they steal spirit and faith.

***

Many of the youngsters from inner-city, lower socio-economic background present a very interesting study in personal drive and discipline. They almost have to be "loners." Consider the peer pressure from their classmates, (or, their "corner mates") to ignore school. It is doubtful many of these youngsters are encouraged to participate on their school teams by their peers, let alone succeed in the classroom. It seems those young men who succeed in academics as well as athletics are very unique young men with a special sense of their individual worth. I have often thought it would be interesting to give these youngsters a battery of personality tests and see what traits they have in common.

***

Winning a game is important. It may keep a group of people employed and provide the players with a source of pride and accomplishment. These are among the material aspects of coaching. But in the long run, for the real worth of coaching, I believe wins and scores aren't too important. As pain can be forgotten so, too, can wins. You can't save them up to tide you over. Games and scores are forgotten or recalled on specific occasions with effort. The real and lasting score is the young men who have been through your program. If they have learned other values through your efforts, then that is lasting and meaningful. Honest participation can be a part of helping these young people develop successful habits, and can help the participant to truly "know himself." This leaves a lasting glow, a personal fulfillment which will last and last and last.

***

Violence in the game and among the fans is a concern to many in the field of athletics. I believe this is the result of the alienation between fan and star. Because of players salaries, life-styles, etc., the average fan has lost the "our team" feeling and rather looks upon the athlete as a display of talent. When that talent doesn't perform as the fan thinks it should then the fan becomes hostile. He looks upon the athlete as an entertainer more than as an "entertaining competitor."

***

Our mobile society has eroded the territorial roots we used to have. In the eyes of the fan, the home team is more "them" than "ours." So when things aren't going well there is hostility that "they have failed us". There is a detachment in loyalty toward players on the home team.

***

Some of these same conditions exist on the playing field. Salary differences, attention, and outside advantages all tend to arouse hostile feelings among some players toward others. It is a rare high salaried player who can walk the tightrope of stardom, financial superiority with fan and player acceptance.

***

Women have enjoyed one great advantage in human relations. Besides using their minds they are allowed the luxury of feelings and emotions. Though the male would like to think the female thinks with "heart more than mind," it is really a rationalization for the structured male conduct that dictated that it wasn't manly to cry from hurt, fear, compassion, or joy. Fortunately, there is an understanding and movement afoot to tumble these false barriers. An advantage of athletic participation is the opportunity to express emotion. . .both happy and sad.

***

It has been females and athletes who could "think <u>and</u> feel!" Athletics is among the very few areas where men can share emotional intimacy.

***

Practice should be geared to two mental outlooks: build confidence in the "team personality" believing they will be successful at what they do and work in practice in anticipation of pressure and adversity.

***

Benjamin Disraeli said of statistics "there are three kinds of lies: lies, damn lies and statistics."

***

Be a leader or be a follower or get out of the way . . . or at least be quiet.

***

One doesn't practice for fun. . .rather for some strong personal need or a long range, sometimes undefined, goal.

***

Leadership roles, at whatever level, have one thing in common. It is not primarily that of motivating subordinates to succeed, rather the one common denominator is <u>overcoming obstacles</u> so the subordinates have an opportunity to succeed.

***

Overcoming obstacles is the common denominator of all leadership roles.

***

Interrelated, but not interchangeable, a fantasy is near impossible to impossible to achieve, but a dream may become a reality. It depends upon your ability to reconcile the dream into a goal. A goal to be reached has intermediate goals along the way and these goals are reached by performing a series of tasks.

***

I have often thought the cynic was the romanticist or idealist who has been wounded. I have thought the pragmatist a functional idealist. . .one who has not deserted his dreams, but will adjust to the realities without losing sight or hope of the ultimate ideal.

***

In major college football, there are many lightweights who play over their heads for the wrong reasons. Ego, tradition, etc., may cause them to continue to compete on a level that is unrealistic. They really can't compete with the heavy-weights on their own merit, so they become parasites. They must play over their own heads and away from home for the big gate that will keep their programs solvent. A big gate is a big gate and all want to make money. The key question to ask, if you wonder about your program, is whether it can generate enough revenue on its own to keep the program at its present level or not? Must the program seek "big gate" games, and play over its head? Does your team travel to a game where the home team insures a good gate or do they come to you? If you played all your games at home, would you generate the income to maintain your present level?

***

As Jim Larue, a great football coach, always said in staff meetings, "it's a lot easier making suggestions than it is decisions." He was speaking of the assistant coaches, especially the young ones, who had all the answers, but didn't have to make the decisions. With this in mind, I always tried to establish a responsibility for each coach where he had to make the decision on policy or action. It was interesting how many times these coaches, when in a position of suggesting could come up with an immediate answer to any situation, but given even minor responsibility, how they would "second-guess" their decision.

***

It has always struck me funny, how when a certain age is reached a coach is considered too old to coach. This is usually around the fifty-year-old mark. It is thought that they have lost some of their zest for travel, recruiting, etc. Their "juices" have slowed down. In fact, in 1977, among major college football coaches, only 11 percent were fifty or older. Among the pros, it was 39 percent. It would be interesting to see how many politicians over fifty and into their seventies have 'slowed' down in their public appearances, travel, etc. When Gerald Ford was in his late fifties and Vice-President, he made 500 personal appearances in eight months.

***

It has always seemed odd that a major criticism of college athletics is that it takes the athletes more than the minimum four years to graduate--as though that is a great injustice to the educational system and the athlete. However, what percentage of the general student body graduates in just four years? It is about the same as the athletes.

***

If one had to work a part-time job in order to get through college and it takes more than four years we commend him for his perseverance and dedication. We do the same with the person who takes three years to get his master's degree and maybe seven to get his doctorate. The athlete, however, who is truly working a full time job during the season and a part-time job off-season, plus going to school, plus the pressure of the sport should be finished in fours years and is somehow looked down upon by some academics. It isn't logical to expect more from the college athlete than from others in school.

***

I have always referred to the players on our team as "kids." Some were twenty-five years old. To me, it was always a term of affection and a way to divide them from the "old men" coaching. It didn't refer to their maturity, etc., it was a term of "love" yet, the question I was asked over and over was, "why do you call the players, kids?" The questioners thought the players should be insulted. They should be called men. Well, I have thought about it. Calling them "men" might have subconsciously led fans to expect more of them than should be and the ones who were concerned about calling them "men" are the same ones, maybe middle-aged or more, who on game day wear every bit of clothing in their school colors; their cars are in school colors, their homes may be done in school colors and they may even have a toilet seat announcing their Alma Mater. These same people will lose a $10.00 bet on a game and want to fire the coach. I sometimes wonder who the "kids" really are!

***

On one occasion, a minister defended me from the question, he answered that Christ called the Apostles His children, since I wasn't made God's equal, but in His image, I could call the players "kids."

***

Repression incites revolution, revolution incites chaos and chaos incites anarchy. It not only happens to governments, but to athletic teams.

***

Athletics is a mode of transportation, hoping the rider has learned something by the end of the line so he can walk alone. Was it not former basketball great Bill Russell, who said, "success is a journey, not a destination?"

***

Athletics can take one a long way, but once you get there, you had better be prepared and a universal preparation is education.

***

Every team has a personality and this team personality is the sum total of the individual personalities blending and subjugating to the whole, yet retaining individuality.

***

Discipline is another word for organization.

***

The Coach walks a strange tight-rope. If he is unsuccessful, internal forces stand by and watch for him to be fired. If he is too successful, those same forces react in fear and want that success thwarted. If institutions believe athletic mediocrity is the measure of a good program then it is fair to assume the institution has the same academic goal.

***

Character and personality aren't the same. Your character displays itself when no one is looking.

***

To feel life one must feel emotion; to feel emotion one must become involved and that means to dare, and to dare risks failure. "Far better to dare and fail than to be among those timid souls who never dare at all." One may dare in many areas. . .and athletics is certainly one of them with a daily tally.

***

When a dream invades the mind the only way it can come true is for the mind to then invade the dream.

***

Psychologists say that the ability to concentrate on detail is an acquired characteristic--something a coach sure better acquire.

***

In 1968, Chuck Jarvis, the army fullback, carried the ball 210 times without a fumble--a tribute to concentration.

***

Victory demands a price for its reward.

***

Big sporting good companies are giving millions of dollars to prestiege collegiate athletics programs so the companies' logo is displayed on the uniform and television. As an athletic director at a Division III college I resent purchasing gear from them knowing the price I pay is subsidizing schools who have millions of dollars in income and we struggle to provide for our teams.

***

It amuses me when parents say their wayward kid is being influenced by a bad crowd. I wonder if that kid is the bad crowd . . . bet other parents think so.

***

In part, today's societal problems are the residue of the social revolution of the '60's. Standards eroded and taboos evaporated. The revolution did not replace the old order with new, just discarded it leaving a social vacuum.

***

Power may be an aphrodisiac; it can also be addictive that is a slave to a fix.

***

Seeking greener pastures isn't always a lack of responsibility. It is the curiosity imbued in our genes that drive our species to new horizons. However, some folks seek the greener grass because they didn't water the old.

***

With focus and effort many people rise above their circumstances, while others never reach them.

***

The biggest threat to today may be yesterday. Yesterday's failure may be today's surrender; yesterday's success may be today's complacency.

***

There are those who give more thought to enemies than friends.

***

My wife would tell me if I loved her as much as I did the players, we would have the world's best marriage. As I think back, I would dismiss the comment, but never did say she was wrong.

***

A long-time friend of mine was the ultimate optimist. One year his team went 1-10. After the season I saw him and asked how his team had done. His answer, "we won all but ten."

***

We would tell our wayward players that they have put themselves in a closet while their life was outside waiting for them. If they didn't exit soon they would be locked in without a key.

***

Calling a company on the phone can be an electronic jigsaw puzzle. You call, a machine answers. The machine gives you a menu via number to push. You push another set of numbers. Could this go to infinity? Then, after it's all done and you don't match a number to your need, then you start again to see what might fit. I find myself being polite to a machine and rude to a person - - - don't know which is what.

***

However, I have developed a break-through of my own. As soon as the machine answers, push the "0" button. You'll get an operator right away who'll transfer you where you want to go.

***

The other side of the coin: soon after the 2000 Super Bowl Ray Lewis, the Baltimore Raven linebacker was alleged to be involved in a double-murder. He was arrested and charged. The charges were eventually dropped. From the time he reported for practice in July 2000 through the entire season the legal ordeal was the center of Ray Lewis coverage. After the 2000 season, he was named NFL's Defensive Player of the Year, followed by the MVP of Super Bowl XXXV. I offer the possibility this never ending redundancy had him playing under a microscope and as a result aided him in his football recognition because he was so carefully observed.

***

Folks, national leaders included, can be highly intelligent but lack wisdom. If they have both intellect and wisdom and embarrass themselves, would be fair to say they lack will power? Worse, it may be a character flaw. Such a flaw can be suppressed for a time, but never can be exorcised.

***

Numerous times, having to make choices I would get advice to "listen to my heart." The dilemma is then compounded because I am unable to decipher which voice is my mind and which is my heart.

***

At the conclusion of the 2000 football season, a wonderful lady retired as secretary to the head football coach at Wake Forest University. Mary Parsons served eight football coaches over a thirty-three year span. Beyond the plethora of duties she had, she was a source of support and friendship. Not a single coach, arriving or departing, had anything but affection for her.

***

Eight coaches in thirty-three years, that is about a tenure of four years per coach. Wake fired me after five years, so by their employment standard, I was above average. (I feel better now)!

***

Spousal abuse exists and is somewhat beyond my understanding. Men subject far more physical abuse upon women than vice versa, but vice versa does exist. Women perpetuate more mental and verbal abuse toward men, but it isn't an exclusive prerogative. Male violence and the effort to dominate, to my way of thinking, isn't the woman leaving . . . rather the fear that the woman can survive without him . . . that would be the crusher to the abuser. Not only does the woman leave . . . but flourishes. To him, that may be the ultimate diminishment.

***

Pope Pius XI said, "Spirit must dominate technique." Teddy Roosevelt, "It isn't the critic who counts, but the man in the area." Neither was speaking about athletics, but both statements sure speak of athletics.

***

Manifestations of our society . . . Gratification now! Results now! Success now! Technology was to lighten the burden on humankind. Instead, it has become an ever-intruding and oppressive force in many lives.

***

Running up scores to improve to improve placement in the football polls is a reality, but certainly not a tool to further mutual respect and sportsmanship. In the football game between Texas Christian University and Southern Methodist, during the 2000 season, the game was sealed for TCU at the end of the third quarter. TCU ran up four more TD's in the fourth, seeking to move up in the BSC standings.

***

As mentioned, in 1999 Notre Dame took an eight million dollar income loss from post-season play by losing to Southern California. In 2000, if they had lost, it would have been a thirteen million smack. That amount of money compromises many educational and ethical principles.

***

The pressure on coaches to win reared its head in the 2000 season with the coach at Arizona State getting fired and the University of Arizona coach resigning under pressure. Within the past few years, both were up for Coach of the Year and their teams in the thick of a number one poll ranking.

***

In the pursuit of television dollars, followed by the need to win eight games for the big pay bowl games, colleges less and less can claim football is part of the educational schematic. There are situations where the institution and sponsors are like pimps, the team a trick and the fans the johns.

***

Coaches not honoring contracts, walking out on a signed agreement . . . then why shouldn't the athlete walk and turn pro before his eligibility has expired? Don't expect him to put loyalty to the institution above millions and millions of dollars.

***

With two parents working we have developed almost a generation of "latch key" kids who have video games parenting them. And, the parents, when able to be home in a family situation they are prisoners of technology. The bottom line is the kid is still alone even when the parents are home.

***

The home used to be the respite and refuge of a day's work. But no more! More pressure, more hassle, overwhelming information provided instantaneously and often instant response is expected. It has spilled into day and night - - - no wonder there are all kinds of "rages" running rampant.

***

With the speed of communication, the world has grown smaller, but not necessarily closer. Technology has isolated the individual. Relationships are becoming more and more abstract.

***

There is a hypothesis put forward that one could live their entire life without having another person participate in their lives. Work, banking, entertainment, ordering food - - - all could be done as long as the electricity doesn't go out. But that barrier has been bridged. It is now easily possible to be with someone and be alone it is called - - - a cell phone.

***

Look around. There are couple sitting in a relaxed setting; one is on the cell phone - - - the other looking into space. Though with someone - - - still alone.

***

In the car in traffic or speeding down the highway, walking along the street, riding a bike, carrying their baby - - - on the cell phone. What is that important? Who is that important? So important that the potential for bringing harm to others is real. And in public places people sitting together talking, can be heard but the content of the conversation not. But one guy on a cell phone and everybody in the place is a party to the conversation. If not by physical proximity, then by atmosphere my peace has been intruded upon.

***

On occasion, when rage has overcome me, when the phone conversation is concluded I offer my advice based on the one sided conversation I was forced to be involved with.

***

Coaches with agents extracting million dollar contracts in the structure of a university almost seems obscene. Buyouts by the institution for an aborted contract, buyouts by a coach to leave early - - - all parties seem to be doing pretty well, I wonder how the assistant coaches are fairing? Is the head coach protecting his staff as well as himself? After all, they are doing the coaching. The head coach can be fired but have enough money to take care of him for the rest of his life - - - the assistants, if they are lucky may get three or four months salary when let go.

***

Early in my high school coaching career I became aware there was a split between the coaches and other teachers. Contributing to that, I believe, was the separation of the physical education facility from the main building; the physical education attire of sweat suits, (no running suits in those days), and most of the coaches would work out during lunch. We initiated a policy that each day a coach would attire himself as the others on the faculty and have lunch with them. No, not talking sports, rather to demonstrate our interest in things beyond sports and to establish a rapport.

***

The general theme was continued at the college level. We would find out what time a large group of the faculty would be together on a coffee break. One of the coaches would join them, building rapport and surprise a few with the fact that the coach was not an idiot savant.

***

A practice increasingly being implemented, after a poor season, is the head coach firing part or all of his coaching staff with some inane comment such as, "the changes were made because the program needs to go in a new direction." Wow! He's the head coach and is responsible for the old direction. His assistants coached in the direction he had determined. If he is going in a new direction, then why is the staff less able than he to coach in the new direction as well? Maybe it's just a cop out, deflecting the pressure on him and putting it on the staff.

***

While the head coach can now concentrate upon his investments his assistants, many with young families, hope they will get a few months pay to help the transition in their lives.

***

All of a sudden coaches who don't have agents and million dollar contracts and who are not celebrities, who are more "off Broadway," than the "great white way," are expected to succeed at the same level as the headliner programs. And by some perverse reasoning it spills into high school expectations and some trickling into Pop Warner.

***

It is amazing how the human body can re-generate itself. Every now and then, when I do get my hair trimmed, and look in the mirror right after, it is shocking to see how my ears have grown. Just because of a haircut.

***

With the constant ebbs and flows of living, the water is always churning. Yet, there finally comes a point where the churning subsides and we can see the calm of the surface below. If we could see that calm earlier in life we might have better coped with the turbulence.

***

If nature controls earth and life on it, it may be God doesn't pay too much attention to the day-to-day activities of life on earth. When judgement comes maybe God pushes a button on the heavenly technology system and an entire life is displayed on a screen. Just a thought . . . not a premise.

***

Imagine the celestial computer system with the entire universe for storage. Earthquakes, drought, cyclones and the like, maybe . . . just maybe, it is a result of the heavenly computers crashing.

***

Not too long ago an allegation came to light that a high school coach was to receive $200,000 if he was able to get one of his players to attend a specific college. True or not true, shenanigans go on. Not being a lawyer, but on the face of it, I would suggest every state legislature pass a law that any external illegal inducement proffered to a coach or athlete be prosecuted as a bribe. If the school, coach or kid is not involved, then leave them out of it. Get the culprit!

***

Tomizo Isumi has been directly involved in Japanese football as a player, coach and administrator for thirty-five years. He spent three seasons on the Wake Forest staff in the mid-70's. Recently, I was attending the Japanese national championship game in Tokyo with him as he passed along an interesting comment. He said in all his years, he has never seen players get into a fight or challenge an official's call. I checked with some other long-time Japanese football people and they echoed the comment. To them it is a matter of their personal honor and respect towards others.

***

There are those who believe you learn from losing but winning teaches you nothing . . . only makes you "feel good." I reject the premise. Yes, losing might lead to more thought and evaluation of one's performance. It also breeds doubt, anxiety and loss of confidence. Winning may feel good . . . but it does just the opposite of losing in terms of confidence and outlook.

***

We used to insist while coaching on the field, when a coach instructed a youngster in regard to technique or assignment that he talked to the player, but loud enough that all others in the group hear and listen. It re-enforces those that know and can teach one who doesn't, thus reducing the redundancy of instructing one player at a time. It saves precious time and keeps the whole group involved.

***

The Second Down

Discipline and teamwork are synonymous, each doing his part and on time. This works much like a family with all parts interdependent.

***

It is amazing how often those most militant about their Christianity fail to practice the most important aspect. . .tolerance towards others. Sometimes called charity.

***

"Victory killers" in a football game are rather obvious. They are dead ball penalties, turnovers, the long bomb, missed assignments, goal line intensity, and failure of the kicking game or, maybe the other team has better players.

***

Good situations create more fine coaches than the opposite. Penn State, Notre Dame, Alabama, Michigan, Ohio State, Oklahoma, Texas and on and on. . .their not being good teams through the years have been the exception, regardless of who the coach might be.

***

Losing leads to frustration, insecurity, misplaced aggression, and loneliness. Both winning and losing have one thing in common: reinforcement! One is positive, the other negative and each tends to perpetuate itself.

***

Somewhere it was said, "courage is the backside of love." It seems love may be the backside of compassion. Love can be selfish; compassion is concern without strings. Compassion may well be the purest of human emotions.

***

Offensive plays are made up by coaches, but executed by players in a scrimmage, to find out what plays the coaches devised that the players believe in, the coach gives only a down distance and field position. Let the quarterback call the play. That will tell you what the team believes will work.

***

Nature is God's plan for the earth, the sea is nature's laboratory and mountains nature's spires of worship.

***

It is interesting to note the coach who will not tolerate a player breaking a rule, while the coach himself may break them with impunity.

***

Exploitation is often a misused word. In itself it isn't evil. We often exploit each other; as long as both parties understand this, it is fair. The school pays for an athlete's education; in turn, the athlete plays for the school. That is mutual exploitation. . .this for that. We, as coaches, had better not cheat the athlete. . .that is negative exploitation.

***

Athletics' Four Horsemen of the Apocalypse: recruiting, boosters, inflation and the media.

***

The Apocalypse of Coaching: discipline, injury, drugs and lawsuits.

***

Television on the sideline has made players more clown than performer. It distracts them and the fan from the game.

***

Something is wrong with the hiring process. A coach is hired by a committee of "non-athletic" people charged with protecting the academic integrity of the institution. Most of them know as much about selecting a coach as a coach does about selecting an instructor for med school. When it comes to retaining a coach, they give no voice nor attempt to protect the coach. They slither away in the security of their tenure. The coach is hired by aesthetics and fired by an animal pack.

***

Grades versus test scores in admission is a battle. It would seem grades demonstrate performance and tests demonstrate potential. Most will agree performance is a reality. The athlete with approximately 1000 on the boards, but only fair grades is the frustrating problem. He was "smart" enough to get decent grades in high school. But often not disciplined enough to study in college.

***

<u>Traits</u> and <u>qualities</u> aren't the same. <u>Traits</u> are somewhat inherent though, with realization and thought they can be modified. <u>Qualities</u> can be acquired.

***

Among the most important traits a coach can have is mental toughness and the vital qualities of integrity and loyalty to school, coaches and team.

***

Camaraderie is the ingredient that holds a team together and makes the end of a career so difficult to admit and adjust to.

***

Law and justice are not synonymous. Law is conceived as a uniform system for the application of justice. It now seems law has evolved into a system to circumvent or erase justice.

***

Each year our team visited the crippled children's hospital. Our players went to cheer the handicapped kids. Our players always went with apprehension and doubt; yet without fail, the players have left inspired. I believe the spirit of the children helps us more than we ever help them.

***

If a coach would ever sit in the stands and hear the viciousness and hostility of some fans, it would be doubtful he would coach again. Tolerance, support and understanding are not the qualities found. . .many truly wish him harm.

***

An assistant coach going after a head coaching job has a better chance than a former head coach going for an assistant job. The reason: the head coach has established his own reputation; his strengths and weaknesses are known. The assistant coach, being picked as a head coach has nothing of his own established, only the perfection as expounded by others. It is the known versus the intrigue of the unknown.

***

The coach's job is to see a player is not exploited and to look out for him when he is not mature enough to look out for himself.

***

Ingratitude seems a human prerogative. . .or compulsion.

***

Recruiting, as sales, is to find the prospect's fears and areas of apprehension, then remedy those areas. The recruiter must listen, acknowledge, probe, and respond.

***

There is a difference between using speed and relying on speed. The former creates problems for the opponent; the latter is used to overcome one's own errors.

***

The trouble with success is that you try to live up to what you have become rather than what you were that got you where you are.

***

True, during a contest, a few referees have been informed of their origins and perversions and some, who could wear a cap, striped shirt and whistle, could go on "What's My Line," and no one would guess what they did.

***

Man is the most sophisticated computer. He provides the data to the computer, that computer provides information, then we depend upon man to make a choice.

***

In both the print and electronic media we are constantly exposed to celebrities promoting a product. It is upsetting that an extremely well-paid individual gets a lot more money for doing the commercial, plus free products in order to get some poor souls to part with their hard-earned money to purchase the product with a profit margin large enough to pay the celebrity big money.

***

Would the postal service stop losing money if they fired all those artists who design new stamps and the cost of set-up and printing?

***

A pass-oriented team had better have a strong defense. The offense doesn't use up much time on the clock. Touchdown or not, a passing offense uses about half the time of a run-oriented offense.

***

Today's athlete is more dedicated than those of the past. There are just too many alternatives, constructive and destructive, available to today's athlete for him not to be quite dedicated.

***

Those in the humanities may see athletics as primitive; the scientists sometimes believe theirs is the only true intellectual pursuit. Both have given to mankind and both may be instrumental in its downfall. Athletics may be the core of liberal arts. . .where else does one learn more about self and maybe life?

***

In athletics there is much in the way of ritual. The danger of ritual is in its becoming form without substance. Religion, too, can fall into this trap.

***

The human condition drives many to wash their hands in innocence or wring them in despair; unfortunately, neither leads to change. The wringing of the hands leads to a loss of self-respect and personal degradation.

***

We search for utopia, but will never find it. In time the freedom we cherish and the self-sacrifice that made it so give way to greed and self-indulgence. This erodes the fabric of society; if the erosion endures the society will crumble.

***

Our senses are sometimes deceived. The violinist, Isaac Stern, once said, "Some of my most appreciated notes were never played, but perceived."

***

Every generation has its own personality, fads and problems but with drugs, it is a fad to ruin a life. . .why? Crime increases among the young when little work is available. Every teenager seems to have dollars in his pocket and a car by the curb. Seeing the American Dream on television those without it turn to crime as a way to get a piece of that dream.

***

We all make good decisions and bad decisions. Far worse, leading to no contact with our destiny, is the decision of "no decision." That is the decision of doing nothing until time or circumstance make the decision for us.

***

Often we think a person is doing a bad job and should be dismissed when the real problem may be the manager's fault, putting the person in the wrong job.

***

At one time, a management consulting firm gave a battery of personality tests to our staff. We all rated differently in each of the categories, but one. . .we all rated low in compliance. If you think about it, that seems an area where anyone challenging the pitfalls of coaching would rate low.

***

It seems as though a lot of kids allow their parents to live at home with them.

***

People and teams are generally motivated by pride, ambition, or fear.

***

An atheistic state won't survive because it puts a lid on the human spirit. Though it tries, an atheistic state can't be a substitute for a Supreme Being.

***

In business or coaching, I prefer task force work to committee decisions. A committee will produce a decision that is the closest it can be to neutral. It isn't aggressive or dynamic. In essence, it is a decision the least offensive to the whole of the committee. A task force can come out with a series of alternatives in a rank order and the manager then makes the decision.

***

I have often thought a committee decision is a way for the manager and the group to avoid responsibility and Roberts Rules of Order is a way of ensuring the process of dilution.

***

Regardless of our pre-game prayer, it seems as though God is prejudice. On Saturday, He always seems to favor the team with the big, fast kids.

***

Good operates by a set of principles. Good feels it is universally honored and it takes a long time before it is realized that the principle isn't universal. This provides evil with a head start.

***

Mental toughness isn't mean and cruel or making difficult decisions. Mental toughness is the ability to cope with numerous problems, duties, and interruptions coming almost simultaneously without being overwhelmed.

***

No matter what one says, game officials have made poor calls that have cost a coach a job. I sure have had some whose competency could be questioned. . . but not their integrity.

***

Many object to the large salaries earned by some college coaches. It is especially offensive to some academicians and on the surface there may be good reason, but two factors should be taken into consideration. First, a long time ago the academics drummed athletics from their midst and secondly, at many schools the coach is a personality and entertainer. As educators there are many overpaid coaches; as entertainers most are underpaid.

***

Watergate criminals are better paid than coaches and often are more welcome on the coach's campus than the coach is.

***

The entertainer (coach) is at the beck and call of a thousand masters. He doesn't need a medical check-up each year, he needs his strings checked so the puppeteer doesn't get them entangled.

***

One time I was asked if, when I went into coaching, I thought I would be another "Bear" Bryant or Woody Hayes. If I was at Alabama or Ohio State, they would be wondering if they would be another Chuck Mills.

***

Delay is decay in preparation for anything.

***

Each of us has a true self-concept and most often it is quite different than we appear or how others may perceive us. It may not be as confident as it seems.

***

Encouraging the athlete with talent who is underachieving is a delicate task. Telling him how good he could be may be the "kiss of death." He may not know what you know and as a result may fear to try.

***

There are those who can achieve, but feel more secure in not trying. They would rather be chastised for not doing as well as they could, than to try and not do as well as you think.

***

Failing to try because of a fear of failing is already failure.

***

The manager often has little time to do the tasks that made him manager. His time for such is minimized. The manager's role is then to see that others achieve success.

***

The human spirit is moved by great talent in any field, providing they understand the talent.

***

I read someplace, "What I am you taught me. . .I am your child."

***

In athletics, both the coach and athlete must make Blas Pascall's, "Leap of Faith."

***

Rules and regulations governing the academic eligibility of the athlete were not created because of the intellectual inferiority of the athlete but rather to protect him from exploitation.

***

The tools of power need not be liked, just used but not abused.

***

Government should be a lead blocker, clearing the way for the individual to work, save and enjoy in security.

***

One's ultimate goal shouldn't be to be the best, just the individual's best.

***

Many extol the joy and electricity of winning, but there is more, winning is hard work, very hard work. Losing is easy. Just don't work hard enough to win.

***

The hostile fan is an exploiter of the weakness of others and not themselves.

***

Potential can be lethal to those who don't exploit it and others who put faith in it.

***

Man and man-made institutions are perishable. It begins with selfishness.

***

Leadership is an innate trait. There are various ways leadership is demonstrated, but it is there. If one doesn't lead in a positive way, the leadership will be negative. But lead will lead.

***

Upon assuming my first major college head coaching job, I sought the advice of my former "boss," Hank Stram. I expected sage advice and deep secrets. He passed along only three words, "Hire good people!" It was the best advice of all. He was talking about people first, coaching second.

***

As best as I could determine, in hiring staff, the three things I tried to attract in the individual and in priority order were loyalty, compatibility, and football knowledge.

***

By others or by ourselves, it is asked, "What do we want out of life?" when the real question is, "What have we put into it?".

***

Charity can come from guilt or ego; love can be selfish, but compassion is pure of heart.

***

Since their release, the hostages held in Iran for 444 days have raised enough money to provide a college education for some twenty children of the eight American servicemen lost in the failed attempt at their rescue.

***

It is always a thrill to see a record broken; not because the old should be broken, or records are "made to be broken." If a record broken endures but a second, think of the thrill, exhilaration and satisfaction of that instant. It lasts one a lifetime.

***

Each record should stand as its own sentinel to that time. Time and distance are constants, but times are not. Technology, technique and facilities change; rules change, so each record stands for its place and time. No record set should be discarded to oblivion; the new standard and the new champion have an eternity of personal triumph.

***

In your staff meetings be sure people may express their opinions. Professional opinions can't be responded to in personal pique. If they are then soon you will receive no opinions.

***

A single source of power may be resentful, fearful and possibly paranoid about any opposition to that power, regardless of how minimal or ineffective it may be.

***

In employing staff, I always wanted to hire coaches whom I thought to be better coaches than me. How else can a staff or team grow and improve? (No doubt, this criteria meant millions were available for a staff of mine).

***

Staff meetings should be for a purpose. To sit for hours stifles creativity and drains energy from the practice field. Set times for meetings so others can organize, but if there is nothing to meet about, don't meet.

***

Early man knew as much about himself as his environment. Modern man knows more about his environment than himself.

***

Sixty percent of all males learn through the visual system.

***

Conversation can clue the system. Comments: "I see." "How does that look?" "I hear you." "Sounds good!" "Wow!" "Run that by me." "Leaves me cold." There are sight, sound and kinetic clues.

***

Maybe the difference between man and animal isn't free-will, rather the animal isn't rational.

***

One must have pride in himself before he can have pride in anything else.

***

A part of coaching is to keep the team agitated. . .not aggravated.

***

If one has interest in what you are doing, then expect some interference in what you are doing.

***

If football doesn't survive, it will more likely be suicide than murder.

***

I have noticed that the player who is doing his job on the field, in the classroom, or in a social setting, may seldom be talked to by the coaches. He is squared away. Much of our energy is spent on the kid who is out of step.

***

Have you noticed, when an athlete digresses on campus, it is always, "Your football player," or "A football player!" Never, "That English major." So, that alone signifies the importance others place on athletics. They acknowledge the classroom may not play any role in values and conduct, but athletics do. Or is it meant as a "put down?"

***

An unofficial observation through the years: When a football coaching staff is let go, it appears the coach in charge of the tape exchange is among the first to land a new job.

***

Sporting events appeal because they have a beginning, the objective understood, the objective achieved. . . all in a few hours. Few other activities have such a clean format.

***

So much of the world is complex and we seem to know more but understand less; sports are simple to understand.

***

It seems technology is twenty years ahead of our ability to cope with it. We may truly be unwitting slaves to technology. . . or maybe not so unwittingly.

***

There are many schools good in both scholarship and athletics. Some of the pursuers of athletic quality, in their immaturity and adolescence, lose perspective.

***

Coaches, in their eagerness to advance in their profession, often leap before they look, taking a position without really knowing the situation. That can be fatal. . .I know, I've leaped.

***

One's heroes are but one's dream of perfection for himself.

***

Individualism, power, aggression, and conquest are passions from ideas.

***

Ideas of good are truth, kindness, beauty, justice, equality and liberty.

***

Love, hate, sympathy, compassion, and prejudice are emotions springing from ideas.

***

Rage is an emotion without an idea.

***

All losing streaks and all winning streaks will end, begin again, and end.

***

Tradition, resources, and athletes make a successful program.

***

The single word to best describe successful team play is "execution!" To achieve execution there are many other words that lead to execution. Some of those words are discipline, conditioning, understanding, emphasis, repetition and talent.

***

What you are successful at you usually work at; emphasis brings success.

***

Perfect strategies are executed by imperfect mortals.

***

Policy requires consistency in dispensation. Human relations in the administration of those policies is not constant. People are different.

***

Reliability and consistency are vital to human relations. As the coach, you are the constant, whatever your personality, but those you deal with are varied.

***

There are segments of the public and especially your educational colleagues who won't like you. Even though they may not know you. Why? You're the coach!

***

If there are lessons in athletics, I'm not sure the starter is the true beneficiary. What about that kid who doesn't get in the game unless you are forty ahead or forty behind and that margin better be at home because he won't travel with you. Does he represent loyalty and dedication?

***

The advent of television and skill of the pros has had an often unrealized negative affect on sports. The fan, without realizing it, sees "athletic genius" perform with the pros and expects the same level of skill down to the Pop Warner teams and all points in between.

***

Every offensive game plan needs three parts. The regular game plan, the catch up game plan, and the desperation game plan. The last is the often ignored one. Don't try to pull the desperate play out of the hat; know what and why the "desperate offense" will be.

***

I have often thought the best measure of a coach's ability is to hold things together in the midst of a losing streak.

***

We learn through one of the following systems: word, sight, kinetic, smell, and taste. In coaching we deal with the first three. If you can identify the learning system you can facilitate teaching.

***

The most rigid of people seem to be closed-minded liberals.

***

Poor coaches! If a team loses consistently, there is a clamor to fire the coach; if the team wins consistently, then there is too much success and the coach must be "put in his place."

***

Not seeing athletics as an art form isn't a lack of sight but rather a lack of vision.

***

Maybe if we promoted athletic contests as the "athletic dance," those from the arts would better appreciate the athletic art form.

***

A quick way to end football violence, so much of which is initiated by the helmet, would be to abolish the face mask. That device alone makes the player feel invulnerable and the helmet a weapon. Require mouthpieces with no face masks and that would eliminate much intentional abuse.

***

Coaching is coaching, regardless of the level. There may be a difference in emphasis, resources and sophistication, but all coaching is the same.

***

The athletic scholarship is as legitimate as any granted for the arts. The athletic grant has more expected than other talent grants, not only is the athlete expected to perform, but to win.

***

It seems half of the world is starving and the other half is on a diet. In the year 2000, half the people of the world will still be without electricity or modern plumbing.

***

To maximize coordination of effort the football staff must have compatible terminology between offense and defense and coordinate the installation of offensive and defensive techniques.

***

In bottom line truth, unreasonable boosters really have nothing at stake in the outcome.

***

In dependency, one party holds power and influence over the other; interdependency, the parties share in power and influence.

***

Creativity is a method of closing the gap between a problem and its solution.

***

The most humiliating indignity of prejudice is that the recipient may believe it has some basis in fact, thus diminishing his opinion of his own worth.

***

A rather extensive survey shows human nature motivates us to do about ninety-five percent of what we do for self-interest. In human relations, we must spend the same amount on other people's problems.

***

Adjust your staff so the least experienced coach has a chance at success. His chances of success will be increased if he is coaching in areas where he has background.

***

Try to place people by their strengths--not yours.

***

Each member of your coaching staff must know the limitations or bounds of his responsibility and authority.

***

Be sure your subordinates know what is expected of them. Then expect them to do it.

***

Goals are fine, but they are reached by performing tasks.

***

The chief administrative job of the head coach is to be sure the program stays on course.

***

If job insecurity is the threat or coercion to force agreement, good people won't be attracted to or remain on the staff. Staff must be permitted to express themselves.

***

Jobs can't be on the line for disagreement. Jobs should be on the line for disloyalty, immorality, or dishonesty. Incompetence may be a reason for discharge, but first should be worked with and an attempt made to over come it.

***

The administrator (head coach) is in that position because he has performed, can keep track of others, and can get others to perform.

***

Keeping track of others requires no leadership, but getting others to perform does.

***

One leads by example; or by direction and edict; or by inspiration; or by loyalty. . .or a combination of all or parts.

***

An effective leader must know his system of leadership. Autocratic, democratic, or delegated authority are the three essential systems of leadership.

***

The head coach must understand his role such as precise identification of responsibilities, parameters of authority and program expectations.

***

To live with honesty can be difficult; without it, impossible.

***

A bad play call, well executed, is a good play; a good call, with poor execution, is a bad play.

***

To improve in practice, the player must endure tedium and possess tenacity. Tenacity is the trait that tolerates the tedious.

***

Each player has a role on the team. He may not agree with it, but he must understand it.

***

A team is primarily made up of average players who are reliable and consistent, supplemented by one or two outstanding players. The average players allow the superior ones to perform and display their skills.

***

Team success comes from the individual pursuit of excellence within the structure of the team effort.

***

Each player must strive to execute his techniques and his assignment better than his opponent plus the mental discipline to endure and maintain his intensity just one second longer and one play longer than his opponent.

***

If a player creates a "will" permitting him to come closer to excellence than his opponent, then he has not defeated his opponent, rather he has created a victory for himself.

***

When the athlete, in practice, makes each effort and repetition as perfect as possible, realizing each effort is a self-test, tedium is surmounted.

***

Tenacity will subdue tedium.

***

One should treat his opponent with the same dignity and respect as he would want shown to him.

***

Robert Louis Stevenson, said, "Be you old or young we are on our last voyage."

***

Change should be made based upon sound assumptions, not just for the sake of change.

***

Resources, scheduling, personnel, and coaching, maybe in that order, are the ingredients of the football program.

***

If a player is successful on one play, each succeeding play the player must prove over and over what was already proven the first time.

***

The result of the last play is the challenge of the next.

***

Satisfaction can not remain constant or complacency will replace acuteness.

***

Four simple rules for play: Know what to do, know how to do it, believe it and <u>Do It!</u>

***

A player must play to the full limits of the rules, but always within them. To cheat may bring a momentary success and at times even a victory, but it is hollow because the cheater will never know if he is the superior performer.

***

Our "Puritan Ethic" historically, may hurt the image of athletics. Athletics, if considered play, would be contrary to that ethic.

***

The mental error is often more damaging than the physical error. The former is a lack of concentration and punishes the team, but is avoidable. The physical error is part of the game, it is an error of action.

***

Success can subvert the role of morality in what man does; in fact success may assassinate morality.

***

For many, there is the feeling that the passing attack is the great equalizer against a superior team; however, for the physically superior team, the pass may be the great neutralizer.

***

Football teams are made up of factors that change annually; to treat these variables as constants can be the downfall of a program.

***

It seems incumbent upon the coach to help develop and promote the self-worth of both staff and players. It is easier to direct, motivate and, in general, deal with folks who think well of themselves.

***

Athletics, within the educational community seems to be under constant attack. This puts athletics in a defensive posture. I am perceived by some as being defensive about athletics; a perception not without merit, but it is based on my unswerving belief in athletics. After all, I have devoted a life to it.

***

There are those who, for whatever reason, have an emotional animosity toward athletics and this reaction can't be changed. It may be wrapped in philosophical jargon but, for whatever reason, it is not without emotional motivation.

***

The objective of the game should be to win, but that should not be the motivating drive to coach or play.

***

Losing brings rejection and winning brings alienation. It is the nature of man.

***

Losing often encourages deviant social behavior by the athletes. The behavior results from the athlete attempting to establish his "macho" image, because he isn't doing it where it is acceptable and expected---in the arena.

***

This same behavior is also nurtured when the athlete feels he is held in low regard by his peers and the faculty only because he is an athlete.

***

A major distinction between high school and college football programs compared to the pros, is off the field. The player's conduct off the field and off-season does have an affect on the quality and perception of the program.

***

Be sure you are right prior to telling one they are wrong.

***

The committee decision ensures a better than stupid decision. . .but it is highly doubtful it will be brilliant.

***

The following is a letter I have always wanted to send to segments of the faculty. . . but lacked the courage:

Dear Colleague:

I am <u>offended</u> at the abuse athletics and coaches are constantly subjected to by colleagues within the academic community. When has athletics attacked other areas of the institution?

I am <u>offended</u> that there are those who think I am less intelligent, less concerned, less compassionate, and less sensitive because I am a coach.

I am <u>offended</u> that there are faculty members who can't be bothered with students; who spend more time off campus than on campus; who use their academic appointment as a way station while pursuing outside activities.

I am <u>offended</u> that there are "academic hacks" who use tenure not as a shield for their provocative thoughts, as it was intended, but as a cocoon to protect them from responsibility for their disinterest and/or incompetence.

I am <u>offended</u> that there are those who diminish the participant in athletics, when it is something the participant is dedicated to and dares to pursue for success or face failure.

I am <u>offended</u> by the elitist attitude of some who have the audacity to presume they can infringe upon the rights and interests of others; who dare to depreciate others by diminishing what they do and in the process erode the self-worth of those individuals.

I am <u>offended</u> by those who infringe, yet aren't infringed upon. By those, who in the name of education, propagate their pettiness and jealousies.

I am <u>offended</u> that so often those portenting they speak for all are only the residue of the radical or boisterous minority seeking platforms for recognition and attention.

I am <u>offended</u> that the purveyors of this erosion do not offer scholarly thought and debate; rather they, themselves, are neither scholars nor researchers of note and in most cases don't speak for the whole faculty.

I am <u>offended</u> when negative generalizations are made or assumed, but any rebuttal or refutation of the claims are ignored.

I am <u>offended</u> that often those applying pressure on coaches are under no pressure themselves. Rather they are using athletics as a way of creating a niche of recognition for themselves.

I am <u>not</u> offended by those who don't understand the commitment and drive of the athletic pursuit; but how dare they attack those who <u>do</u> understand!

I am <u>not</u> offended by those who think athletics not to be sacred; but neither is it sinful.

I am <u>not</u> offended by those who recognize wrong-doing or evil in athletics; nor am I offended by those who call attention to abuses. I am offended when it is not recognized that abuse seems to be an institutionalized human condition, regardless of one's profession.

I am <u>not</u> offended by those calling for reform. I am offended when vindictiveness is the true flag of the reformers.

I believe the athletic academician (coach) is as or more committed, involved, compassionate, sensitive, and demanding toward his students than many other educators.

I believe each student who has gone through our program is a better person for it. I believe they better understand themselves and others. I believe they have dared. In the broader sense of the word education, I believe the participant has an expanded education beyond the routine academic experience. I know he has!

I am <u>offended</u> by those who don't know the definition of education, liberal or otherwise. They appear to be trained in their field, but not educated.

I am <u>offended</u> by those who are unable to recognize athletics as a form of human expression as is music or art or literature or dance.

I am <u>offended</u> by many who refuse to recognize that the athlete is not enrolled in athletics, but in every school of the college and from a practical standpoint, provide many, many dollars to the college and the numbers involved help to ensure the very employment of faculty.

I am <u>not</u> offended at sincere concern or legitimate inquiry if the answers to the questions are considered and if they are reasonably accepted.

I am not <u>offended</u> that there are those who have no interest in athletics or think them a waste of time. As they should not be offended when there are those who may think the same of their endeavors.

I am not <u>offended</u> that there are those who can't recognize the expression of joy or human spirit as manifested in athletics.

If the recorded history of man and his institutions were displayed as a mountain mural, athletics would be among the highest peaks.

I am proud and find great satisfaction in the avenue I have chosen for my life. I do not believe it has been uneventful, wasted or unfulfilled. I fear a loss of health may keep me from it. I am angered that what I do will be taken from me by death!

So, please don't offend me. . . or my kind. . .it isn't deserved.

***

Offensive blocking is simple. Know who to block, get off the ball, maintain contact. . .and if you don't know who to block, then do the rest on somebody.

***

The job of the kick-off return wedge is to create a gap in the coverage and this must be done by attacking. The kick returner can't expect all the coverage to be neutralized. He must go without hesitation into a gap.

***

The sadness in attacks upon the value of athletics isn't the damage done to the abstract, rather the attack upon the self-worth of the participants. We all want to think what we do is of value, if only to ourselves.

***

As individuals and families search for their roots, for a football team, its roots are in tradition.

***

Football isn't the most important thing in life when observed from perspective; however, for many young men it is the only lever to direct achievement until they have a perspective.

***

Those faculty members who enjoy the "humaness" in teaching seem to respect the efforts of other people in other areas and feel it has value if others want to participate.

***

An additional unofficial observation, those faculty who are vocal and hostile toward other campus enterprises are usually the same faculty members for whom students have little affection or regard.

***

One thought for sure. . . for the top athlete . . . except in very rare exceptions. . . recruiting starts off as an affirmation of self-esteem, ego and importance. . . and just as often the parents are as euphoric as the kid.

***

In the end it is an ordeal that leads to confusion, harassment and unbelievable pressure. . .even after a decision is made the player and the parents are haunted by second - guessing. What starts as a thrill ends up as a siege.

***

After many years of recruiting for football I have developed some informal guidelines:

"Mills Recruiting Roadmap."

The athlete's mother, had better be on your side. No matter what she says, the youngster knows her preferences and often will honor them. Whenever I ran into a father who said "he'll go where I tell him," we hardly ever attracted the youngster. If the prospect's father tells you his son will go where he says and the father wants him with you, leave the kid alone. You won't get him. The prospect is just at the age of independence and wants to do "his thing" and will not want to be going to school where Dad dictates. He is at the age of rebellion and the father's plan is countered by the athlete. But with the mother, there is a communication and tenderness that transcends many material considerations. Get the mother on your side and it is easy to do . .. know something of your school and its academic program, be sure she knows he will eat and sleep well and above all, you and the school and football staff will be interested in his well-being and will look out for him.

***

The athlete will listen to the recruiting coach, but knows he is selling. The recruit will believe the athletes; they are his peers and are to be trusted. Your present athletes can do more to attract an athlete or lose him than any other factor.

***

For the athlete and the family, recruiting begins as a compliment, but ends as an ordeal. The youngster becomes confused and changes choices day to day. After Mom, in the end, the choice will be made upon his opinion of the athletes he met while being on the campus and his relationship with the coach recruiting him. Since he is confused, he will go to the school where he feels he can trust the recruiting coach and where he liked the players.

***

When a youngster visits the campus it is important to know if the visit to your campus is the first visit he has made. Many youngsters don't know how to conduct themselves. If the first visit, some will be too shy to seek information, others put on a "bravado" act trying to impress. After a few visits, when the youngster visits a campus, "what you see is what you get."

***

When a youngster visits your campus assign a host to him that will be with him the entire time. After the visit ask the host his impression of the prospect, will he fit in or not? What kind of person is he? This will be the most accurate information and measure you will receive.

***

Never tell a player to come with you because he can play for you and not the competition. He regards that as a "put-down" either that your program isn't that good or he isn't that good. A confident player believes he can play for anyone. . .now, if a kid asks you who is coming back at his position or how long are your practices, don't forget him. . .but cool off a bit. He is marginal in attitude.

***

NCAA rules limit visits to 48 hours. Whenever a lad visits for a shorter period of time you fear it isn't enough. On a percentage basis we attracted far more on the shorter visit than the longer one. The quick "in and out' avoids activity gaps.

***

When a prospect visits your campus and consumes his final meal on your campus. . .if he eats like a "pig," devouring everything in sight, he isn't coming. He is loading up and figures he will never see you again. If he eats "normal" then he still has interest and cares about the impression he makes.

***

The candidate's impression of the players we have and a coach he trusts will be two very big factors in his decision.

***

The athlete, in most cases, knows the school of his choice, where he would prefer to go. Then he has a back-up of three or four schools in the event his first choice doesn't take him. Very seldom does a school come out of nowhere and "dazzle" him without his having an already existing interest in that school.

***

The black athlete has a stronger maternal tie than the caucasian athlete, plus being a bit more aloof and suspicious in the initial contacts. His sometimes obvious guarded attitude is the result of this apprehension. It is quite common with the black athlete, when he and his family does trust, it had best be returned in kind or you will have trouble recruiting the next youngster.

***

The admissions office and the athletic department are the two most active recruiting entities on any campus. Often other departments on campus think it isn't their role, their concern or beneath them. Yet, athletes recruited aren't recruited as athletic majors, only as participants, athletics recruit for every academic discipline on the campus. This recruiting effects numbers in the academic discipline and can impact the number of faculty, courses offered, funds allocated, etc.

***

Having no children of my own, I believe I placed an unfair yoke on the players on our teams. They (players) became my children and as a result maybe I expected too much of them, not allowing them to grow and even transgress. What they did or did not do was maybe too personal to me.

***

Athletes don't get from athletics nearly as much as they bring to it. Those things we pontificate athletics build are nothing more than qualities and traits imbued in the youngsters who prevail. Athletics provides the catalyst for their display.

***

What the athlete gets from athletics is camaraderie, friendship, affections and life-long memories. When the sports career is over, the game isn't missed, rather the things missed are the trappings and associations.

***

Most coaches believe they have had an impact on the lives of their players. I would like to believe if former players do well in life, I had a role in it. What about those who do poorly? But I am not sure the premise is true. What may be more truthful is the coach may keep a young life on direction and under control until the athlete is ready to take charge of his own destiny.

***

It seems ludicrous that the pro players' contract settlement includes adjustment pay to assist the player to make the transition from his pro career to a non-football profession. After all, they say, he is years behind his non-football peers in getting started in a career. They don't mention he may be a lifetime or two ahead of those peers in money earned.

***

My observation leads me to believe the vocal, hostile faculty toward athletics, many times are the same faulty members who teach with indifference toward their students. They are rigid, impersonal and seem not to bring enthusiasm nor zest to their courses or students.

***

It's not the starting lineup that counts, it is the one that finishes.

***

Coaching "burnout" is intriguing. If burnout is suffered, it doesn't mean one isn't good at coaching, it means it isn't enjoyed.

***

The ultimate vanity among coaches must be the one who wins honors one year, loses the next, soul searches and determines he will give up coaching because he can't understand why the team lost. That isn't martyrdom, it is an ego unwilling to compete or give credit that others, too, may be good coaches.

***

A coach fired suffers a diminished ego, but it won't shatter a good coach's confidence.

***

It must be noted by the coach that social dynamics are a primary motivation for athletic participation. The coach, utilizing this need, can encourage social awareness and responsibility among the team members.

***

A team with "bad actors" who are not challenged and controlled will attract more of the same and then the program is out of control; the good kids you want on the team will leave. Conversely, a team comprised of sincere, dedicated athletes squeeze the negative ones out. They will either get in step or withdraw, they know they don't belong.

***

Any organization that promotes their leaders from within gives hope to all members of the organization. However, the one promoted to lead changes from a colleague to a superior, this can lead to alienation from the group.

***

A new coach taking over a new position certainly has his own ideas and wants the stamp of his "program" to take hold, but beware: analyze and evaluate, before changing everything. Know what was done well by the previous staff and it may be in order to keep it in place. The more kept in place, the easier the transition for the athletes.

***

The library and the gymnasium, they are the same! Some use only one; some use one more than the other and a few use neither. One building exercises the mind; the other the body. One taxes the mind, one refreshes it. One exposes the mind to principles; the other puts them into practice. Each is important to the other. The individual is not a whole with one and the other a void.

***

Depression is to despair what elation is to exhilaration. In that sense, victory has a more lasting affect on one's well being than a loss.

***

The term "killer instinct" in athletics is misleading. It is a misnomer. In athletics it is a substitute that really means knowing how to win. Effort, concentration, knowledge, determination, execution; these are the main components of the "killer instinct" in athletics.

***

A newly hired coach usually is selected to compensate for the shortcomings of his predecessor. The new coach is replacing real or perceived weaknesses. He must keep in mind he is bringing his own shortcomings to the program and if his program fails the next coach will be selected to compensate for those shortcomings. The unbroken circle.

***

The just hired coach will be greeted with open arms and enthusiasm. But remember, he is in contact with those who wanted change. Not known by the coach, within every constituency of the program the new coach has opposition, those unhappy with the change in the first place; maybe unhappy the coach of their choice wasn't selected or they were excluded in the selection process. Be aware, the road isn't that smooth.

***

Those players who have been playing are apprehensive of the new coach, their security has been shattered. Those players not playing are usually happy, they feel they will have a new start. Security and confidence are most important to a player. The new coach erases this.

***

A thought: if major college football is entertainment and the revenue is vital, then it may be worth considering to pay the coach according to seats sold. Pay the coach so much per seat sold, the better the home attendance the more his salary. When the attendance drops so does the salary. This system would also pay the coach according to the program's level. It's a thought.

***

The emphasis on winning can never be diminished in competition; it is a human condition. What can be diluted is the stigma of defeat. Victory is the goal and reward for talent, effort, cooperation and sacrifice, but it isn't always achieved. It is the strived-for conclusion, but reality doesn't mean one will always be rewarded as they deserve. Losing is not winning. . .nor is it failure.

***

Every coach coming into a situation talks about building a winner. There is more to it, but winning is wanted and most easily understood by constituencies. It is the easiest to articulate even if not the only objective the coach has in mind.

***

Keeping things in "perspective" is a thoughtful way of saying, "Do it my way!"

***

If the N.F.L. wants to sign undergraduates, but wish to avoid wholesale raiding, the solution is simple. . .any undergraduate signed must be given a no cut contract with a return to school clause or the salary is reduced.

***

In eleven years of keeping records in Division I, our coaching staff put in an eighty-four hour week during the season For the entire year the coaching staff had only eleven weekends where they were free on Saturday and Sunday.

***

A survey made a few years ago showed the average tenure of a major college head coach in his career was 5.2 years..

***

A basic component for a successful football program is tradition; a component for a successful team is morale.

***

Assistant coaches jockeying for promotion can be be very disruptive to a staff. A way to avoid this distraction is for the head coach to set a policy at the outset that is clear to all. Among the policies:

1. If more than one assistant on the staff go for a job elsewhere, the head coach will support the senior member applying.

2. If a coach on the staff departs, tell the assistants whether the plan is to promote from within or bring in an outsider. In this way the coaches can adjust or seek other employment. But above all unnecessary anxiety is averted.

3. Graduate assistants really try to establish themselves. They should be told if a graduate assistant is selected as a regular coach, responsibility and seniority will be the sequence.

***

By doing this the aspiring coaches can concentrate on football and not politics, and avoid the most fatal blow of all, when the head coach leaves and more than one of the assistants wants the job. The staff had better get together and back one man and one man only. If more than one applies, more often than not they neutralize each other and all are knocked out of the box.

***

Sometimes, if we think about it, when a youngster has aspirations to be a professional athlete, the only training ground he has is intercollegiate competition. To be able to participate he must attend college and take prescribed courses in prescribed numbers in a prescribed period of time. We don't require this of one who wants to be an artist, dancer or musician. From that standpoint we demand more from some youngsters to pursue their vocation than others.

***

Academics can teach you to appreciate man's development and culture. It can teach you to learn how to learn. It can teach you how to earn a living.

***

Athletics can teach one about self and give one practical experience on "how to live," to work with others and be in competition with others while maintaining civility.

***

Those internal critics of athletics and athletic recruiting would have a different opinion if they were thrust into the responsibility for the college "head count." On each campus where I have been, registrars, admissions officers and alumni officials were most supportive of athletics and recruiting. . . and for professional reasons. The critical faculty members on a campus should realize that athletic recruiting can have a direct effect on their employment and that of their colleagues.

***

For most every player, regardless of the commotion and numbers and being a team game, there are quiet. . .almost terrifying moments of being absolutely alone. . .even in the noise and in the midst of others. This is especially true in those few moments before the game. . . there is anticipation and fear of the unknown. It is abject loneliness. It is at those moments one's spirit and mortality join together. They are private, secret moments. Though with others, one is isolated.

***

Division I football is fully exploitative and at times insensitive to the needs and welfare of the players. The team must be successful and entertaining in order to attract fans who bring dollars. They must serve their public.

***

Programs at a lesser level can serve the athlete more readily and at the same time provide entertainment, but need not be exploitative. Gate receipts aren't the financial life blood of the program.

***

It is often said that coaching is a "young man's game." Paul Bryant, Woody Hayes, George Halas, John Wooden, Marv Harshman, Ray Meyer, Casey Stengel and many more put that perception to rest. The fact is, it seems a young man's game because men with power fire the young men before they can reach an older age in their profession.

***

Success is seldom accidental. It must be dreamed, believed, planned and achieved.

***

One cannot purchase respect, affection or love. These are qualities that must be earned and given freely. One trait that is an exception is loyalty. It may be earned and willingly given, but it has an added dimension. Loyalty can be purchased. An employer, by providing one's livelihood has a right to expect and receive loyalty.

***

The recent division of football among colleges and universities, in order to establish their own destiny regarding intercollegiate athletics is a good thing. It isn't final and will progress through further evolution. But within this framework, a school studies its resources, competition, and objectives and can place itself in an atmosphere for somewhat equitable competition.

***

Though there are exceptions, in general Division II and III have established programs within the educational and financial criteria of their situation. In many cases Division I institutions compete on the Division I level, not within their capabilities, but in spite of them.

***

The drive by some already in Division I to maintain that status and the criteria established for Division I ranking is not at all realistic, but it does show the ego and pressures placed on the marginal institutions. There are Division I schools, with stadiums of 20,000 averaging 12,000 per game attendance, who are now expanding their stadiums to the required 30,000 seats. Why? So they can say they are a Division I member.

***

In the long haul, it will be the Division II and III institutions who will be the strong, solvent group. The scholarship limit will filter down and has already, so there will be more and better players for all the schools.

***

There are small, private universities with enrollments under 4,000 with limited resources who have athletic budgets over $5,000,000. They can succeed in the financial arena only with very successful teams who are on television and go to bowl games. To do this, some will compromise their standards, or out and out violate the rules for the financial success needed. And to add to this, these smaller schools within strong conferences aren't accepted with whole-hearted support from the other members. Why? Because they receive an equal share of television and bowl revenue as dictated by the conference, but their operation is a handicap to the remainder of the league.

***

A simple illustration would be in home game football attendance. A smaller school, averaging 25,000 per game attendance while all other conference schools are over 50,000 creates a financial drain on the larger schools when playing away, while the smaller college receives a disproportionate share when they travel. In 1978, the big ten averaged 61,149 a game; Northwestern was 19,604. There is quite a difference in paydays. The Southeast average was 56,789, while Vanderbilt was 26,967.

***

A rather ruthless attempt to squeeze the weaker schools from the conference is to raise the minimum guarantee to the visiting team, hoping to make it prohibitive for a continued conference affiliation.

***

The desire to be "number one" or be in the company of those who are, leads to eventual disaster. It will take time and a number of coaches will be sacrificed to the "gods of ego and finance" but eventually, those in charge will have to adjust.

***

Divisions II and III have made that adjustment. They can build their own programs as they want. They can get stronger if they so choose, but regardless, it will be their determination relative to their own evaluation and not dictated by external criteria that isn't their true personality.

***

Division II and III have no less desire for success nor should they make any less effort to be as successful as they can be within their framework. Their great advantage is that they haven't sold their athletic interests to outside forces that have no interest in the well being of the school or student - athlete. They will progress "within" and not in "spite" of their resources.

***

There are very big dollars in major college athletics. In the effort to attract those dollars, major college athletics have become a spectacular extravaganza. Pure show business. The need to be successful only unto itself and all other values become secondary. The tragedy of this goal is that there isn't that many dollars for all. Some must go under!

***

I am certain there are thousands upon thousands who have the intelligence, interest, and ambition to be leaders. What may separate the thousands from the few who achieve may be energy and energy alone. The energy to perceive and to pursue. After the excitement and success of a pursuit, where the energy is generated by the excitement and pursuit, then a new source of energy must be found to maintain the pace. It is often said that maintaining success may be harder than achieving it. Energy is the drive-wheel.

***

For one or for a team, achieving success must begin with a positive self-perception and a belief in what can be done. This intangible is an abstract, while the achievement becomes tangible.

***

Was the opening of colleges to all in the sixties and seventies a true effort to provide an educational opportunity to all. . .or was it some kind of plan to get the revolutionaries and the dropouts off the streets? If it was a plan it seemed to backfire. The college campus gave these zealots a base of operation and a well meaning but impressionable "army" to recruit.

***

It seems some people have intelligence while others have common sense and some have both. The difference between the two, I heard, or read someplace, is "intelligence" is intuitive perception; common sense (or rationale) is "reason by deduction".

***

We all should have great heroes to inspire us, if not to emulate, then at least to keep us aware of the human condition and what one can do. . .the great achievements in human spirit. For me, the group includes no athletes or coaches. . .mine are:

***

Frank Johnson, was a federal judge in Montgomery, Alabama who took on the whole social fabric of the south with the civil rights decisions he made. These decisions cost him many personal tragedies. His was the decision that said Rosa Parks need not sit in the back of the bus.

***

Raoul Wallenberg, the Swedish ambassador, who, with the use of the Swedish Flag, saved the lives of thousands from Hitler's death camps. Germany needed Swedish steel and couldn't afford to alienate Sweden. Wallenberg, throughout occupied Europe, designated property as Swedish Consulates, flew the flag and housed the targets for death.

***

King Christian of Denmark, in World War II, did much the same as Wallenberg. The Nazis, when occupying Denmark, ordered all the Jews to wear a yellow star. The first donning the star was the King himself, thus setting an example that was emulated by many citizens of Denmark.

***

Another kind of hero to me was Arthur Fiedler, late director of the Boston Pops. His contribution was to bring so much good music to so many and through that music he brought joy.

***

Helen Keller, who was an example of personal courage, dedication, and effort and above all had the power of human spirit as manifested by her accomplishments.

***

Included in this list must be the "total person" of the United States of America on the July Fourth celebration of our 200th year. For at least a day we were a healed and healthy America.

***

In order to move up the playing ladder you must do better than the player ahead of you; in order to win, you must do better than the player across from you.

***

Charlie Jones, pro football television announcer for many years, on one of his broadcasts made a great comment, "for a place kicker, life is a continuous audition."

***

When we are knocked down in life we have no choice but to roar back. It is interesting how some will "bounce back" and others will "bounce up." The former keeps going and doesn't capitulate to life, while the latter seems to achieve beyond their former status. Of course others in life just "bounce around" while some never bounce at all.

***

I have always thought it a bit of an untruth telling a new player coming into your program that he is going to be a starter. I think it is fair to say the youngster will have a fair chance to display his talents, and the best will play. It is also unfair to tell everyone that positions are "wide open." I don't believe that. I believe the returning players have earned the right to hold down the starting position in the beginning. They have equity in the position. . .but, if they don't make payments to maintain that equity, there will be foreclosure and the player will be replaced.

***

It has been said that a garden is the coming together of Art and Nature.

***

Life isn't fair or unfair, good or bad, if anything it may be the worst of all. . .indifferent. Life is no more than the environment we have for living.

***

The only admissions officer I want to give special consideration for the entry of the unqualified is St. Peter. . .in my behalf.

***

The SAT's and the ACT's are like the Ten Commandments. Knowing them indicates a potential for doing well, but it is in the performance that it counts. Living by the commandments and earning good grades is performance and that is what pays off.

***

If there is something you think and it has importance, with an effort it may become something you know.

***

Those who are fatalists somehow offend me. It seems a "philosophical" way of "letting George do it." To be a fatalist allows one to avoid prevention, preparation, recouping and thinking.

***

Contact sports are basically games of will.

***

Football has changed from controlled mayhem to a computer print-out. In the end, the computer tells what people did or did not do.

***

Civility is often regarded as a sign of weakness when in reality it is a sign of strength and confidence.

***

Apparent sincerity is always subject to proof. Without proof it is a possible fraud.

***

Many sportswriters are products of the 60's. At the time they may have been dissidents. Many dissidents begin as idealists; when reality hits the idealist and he is unable to adjust, he becomes a cynic. This attitude has permeated the attitude of some sports writers and is manifested in their constant effort to degrade and deflate the athletic entity.

***

The participant in athletics is expected to play by the rules and to play with honor and dignity; the coach, unable to directly participate is expected to coach and teach the game according to the rules and with honor and dignity.

***

The sportswriter is a step further away and acts as the observer for the public. He wants the coaches and players to abide by the rules and be honorable and honest. If that is the role the sportswriter perceives for himself, then it should be expected that he, too, should function within the same standards and guidelines. He has no right to do less and expect more of others and remain in his profession--the tertiary of athletics.

***

Performance is the only way to sustain success. Whether it is a product or a person, coasting only goes downhill. It must be realized that performance may not guarantee success, but it must be executed and continued to attain and sustain.

***

Destiny may exist, but one must also attempt to "grab destiny". One must learn to act in one's own behalf. In a very basic way this is proven everyday. If destiny acted as an independent force without individual participation, there would be no need to shop for food or put gas in a car. . .if it was in destiny's plan it would take care of itself. But gathering food, keeping warm with a fire or whatever, are basic acts of "grabbing destiny." It will help to control one's destiny if assisted by the individual.

***

Goal setting must be realistic. A goal should be someplace between the present reality and the dream. Goals can be the step ladder to dreams, but must be attainable.

***

The coach is sometimes caught in the "never, never land" of being either a policeman or a social worker. If he is too autocratic and unyielding he is considered a martinet and too oppressive. Then again, if he helps or tries to help young people, who often have bodies more mature and experienced than their minds, then he is thought of as too lenient and without control. If the middle road is followed, then nobody knows where the coach stands and where the line of demarcation is drawn.

***

To have success one must remain persistent when frustrated. Many of the weak fall by the wayside when faced with frustration.

***

The "fight or spirit" of the individual or the team can be measured simply. . .will there be a comeback after a setback?

***

There is no question that because of athletics there are unqualified students who are admitted to college. Some of the unqualified students will make it and some have no chance, be it by background and/or motivation. On the other side of the coin, because of athletics a number of students who lack academic interest and possibly maturity will attend college and after a time via osmosis or whatever, they become aware of the value of their education and pursue and complete their degree work. Somehow we can't forget that athletics may be the bait that gets the bite, and a sincere interest in education develops along the way. Though some may gain more than others, even those who fall by the wayside are benefited by the collegiate exposure.

***

If you matter to yourself you will have others matter to you. Others can't matter to you without the first step being self-regard.

***

Freedom in its purest form can be destructive and a seed to anarchy. Freedom has limits. Freedom is limited by the constraints of having a civilized society. Freedom unrestrained can be carried to the point of destruction of others and destruction of self. It can't be practiced in the absolute.

***

There are those who go through life as though they were on a highway with no map. We all go through times when we are on the road, but not sure where we are going. We search for the destination, but that is a lot different than having no destination.

***

A goal is a road sign between the present reality and the dream we are seeking.

***

Leaving football will mean the loss of my last grasp of youth. Fresh hope and excitement every year, bewilderment, the dreams, and the camaraderie will leave my life. All the little boy in me will be a vapor. I'll miss that little kid who has lurked within this aging exterior for so many years.

***

Coaching is the way some of us have chosen to make a contribution to society and a hope to develop habits and values that will serve a lifetime. But it isn't all giving. For the coach the return can be ego-satisfying. . .a chance to "stay young" and the chance to compete within a structure that defines the outcome that day. Coaching can offer high profile adulation and material rewards. . .and high profile condemnation. The return can be forced unemployment at an age when those in other professions are preparing for retirement. Why? Why such a choice of professions? Optimism, confidence, ego, joy of competition and maybe altruistic reasons as well.

***

It is near impossible to ever turn your back on a player, present or past, if they are in need of support and help. . .even when your back <u>should</u> be turned. If you are being used, you will be hurt and disappointed, but you will survive. . .but if you turn your back it may be the one time you have crushed that individual's last hope.

***

Sports writers can be a vicious lot. They often create the clamor that get coaches fired. They can turn a disgruntled few into a blood letting mob if the coach doesn't please them. <u>Sports writers may come as close to anything in our society to having power without responsibility.</u>

***

One may not always agree with the press and a thin-skinned coach may bristle at criticism, but that is a part of the profession. However, a reporter with a personal agenda that may jaundice fairness and objectivity can be tolerated, but when integrity is submerged to satisfy a personal vendetta and the newspaper used as the forum, then that reporter should lose his right to write.

***

A sportswriter has a forum, (the paper) and he has an opinion, but he has no right to turn his back on principle and morality. If a coach transgresses, his scalp is called for. If the writer transgresses, he speaks of the "public's right to know!" Know what? The truth or a lie?

***

Coaches with 70 and 80 percent winning records who are successful and decent men, are being fired. It is depressing and has a ripple effect. Some coaches are so well paid and given so many tools for success that it is quite possible unreasonable expectations are reasonable, but it soon becomes the standard for all and the conditions that surround these expectations aren't universal. Do we disbar lawyers, void medical licenses, fire salesmen, and eliminate stock brokers who are only 80 percent successful?

***

Don't kid yourself, the "scalp hunters" are no different at any level of competitive sports. When they come after the coach. . .they come after the coach. . .beginning in youth sports.

***

Through athletics, possibly the most important thing we can impart to athletes in our charge is a sense of self-respect and self-worth. Yet to do this requires the youngster to do for himself. As coaches and even institutions, this can't be done to them or for them, hopefully the environment is such that the individual will do for himself.

***

A good defense is like water, it will find its own level of consistency. It is a little more difficult for the offense because the defense can adjust and disrupt.

***

"Intellectuals prove you can be as brilliant as hell and not know what the hell is going on," from Woody Allen's film, Annie Hall. Respect and evaluate what the idealist says; it is something to strive for, but don't surrender to it until the environment makes it equitable.

***

Some feel government grants to college students are a form of "academic welfare." Not true because the education achieved provides great returns to the society. This return is the expectation, just as successful performance is the return for the athletic scholarship.

***

The athletic scholarship is an "award" and not a "reward." It is not for value received, but value expected.

***

Athletics can be more abruptly cruel than routine life, but also can be more emotionally reassuring.

***

At times we all need refuge from our loves, as well as the solitude to reflect and appreciate.

***

Taking drugs is like tinkering with a computer that isn't broken. There is no "How To" book included. You are unable to see what you are tinkering with and when finished "fixing" you are "busted."

***

Doing your best is what you control. Being the best may be something others control.

***

Failure is not fatal, and success is not final.

***

The coach had better evaluate his team and develop his tactics accordingly. As in the stock market, it must be decided if it is a Bull or Bear team. Should the team be one that has a reliable and constant return for effort or one that is volatile? It would be quite common to have the offense dealing in one market while the defense invests in the other.

***

There is an old Spanish proverb: "Take what you want, said God, then pay for it later."

***

Bad can thrive because good hesitates to challenge. Just as cold is the absence of heat.

***

Good ideas are common. . .energizing ideas is the test.

***

Coaching situations require different approaches. It is incumbent upon the coach to find what the true priorities and expectations are. What is expounded may not be the realistic framework the coach is expected to achieve.

***

Memory diminishes truth. . .imagination embellishes it.

***

If everyone likes you then you may stand for nothing. For everyone you thrill or energize there are others whom you aggravate and alienate.

***

"Wonder if the going up is worth the coming down?" As a Kris Kristofferson song goes. To fully live life one must make this decision. If it is a natural high of life, then it is worth it. If it is artificially induced. . . maybe not.

***

It was Toynbee, the great historian, who stated that all the great civilizations (Societies) collapsed from within. The savings and loan scandal is an illustration of what can happen. It has more than shocked the country, it has eroded our fabric. It has undermined us. It has robbed the nation of the resources for health care, education, medical research and what else? It has placed a burden on generations to come.

***

I am not the least bit interested if it's Republicans or Democrats or Liberals or Conservatives. These labels are being used to explain the symptom. The disorder is greed, immorality, and incompetence. . .traits of the human species. It has been supported by accountants and lawyers of the same ilk. It is a time for statesmen to come forward. Our political representatives need to be courageous and function to the full extent of the definition of politics and politicians not just self-serving segments. And athletics are evil by comparison?

***

Focus is the essential for consistent success. After a period of time, this focus must be worked at to be maintained. It is the ingredient that negates complacency and erosion. If external factors are allowed to interrupt the focus then multiple aspects of the organization can become unglued. To maintain total focus on the part of the staff and team builds success in the program and this must be maintained for it to continue. Anything that tends to distract and intrude upon this focus will lead to a diminished outcome and it can take a year or two or three for the erosion to be realized and when it is, it may be too late to recover. Recapturing what is lost is more difficult than retaining what is.

***

Athletic participation can provide pleasant memories from the past; the college degree can implement the dream of the future.

***

It is worth considering sending a monthly newsletter to faculty, administration and staff telling about the football program. It could include academic matters of the athletes and honors, philosophy and notes of general interest. There will be faculty or others who will contact you with negative comments such as wasting paper or "who cares?". Don't let that discourage the effort. Most will be appreciative though they may not let you know. The newsletter permits you to paint a picture of your program.

***

If your outlook will permit outsiders to share your program, consider at each home game and possibly on the road, inviting a member of the faculty to spend game day with the team. Have them attend the coaches' final check meeting, the pre-game meal, team meetings, training room, locker room. . .and be on the sidelines during the game. Many depart with a greater realization of the organization, pressure, and intensity that goes into playing football.

***

People repeat rewarded behavior. Don't be afraid to brag about a subordinate's performance. . .not to do so is a matter of insensitivity, insecurity, or both.

***

Solutions to grievances can be more easily resolved if they are included in the process.

***

The thought keeps rearing its head in my mind that education either produces or is the refuge for a disproportionate number of evil personalities. They often justify their viciousness under the guise of academic freedom, or their definition of morality and integrity. It may well be this attitude is nurtured by the lack of realism in their world. They are examples of the abuses that can exist in a well insulated welfare system; in this case it is called tenure!

***

Money corrupts in business, government, education and athletics. In athletics the corrupter is television and the big money it promises. Athletics, in many ways, takes on the role of the "world's oldest profession" with television the pimp, athletics the prostitute, and the fans the trick.

***

The vigilante, who rids the streets of thugs, (as Charles Bronson did in "<u>Death Wish</u>") creates a moral dilemma. An orderly society can't tolerate the vigilante and law must uphold this practical concept, yet Bronson's actions were cheered in the film because they appealed to our sense of justice. Again, law and justice in conflict; however, in the end law must prevail.

***

A new coach taking over a down program is commonly given a five year contract. On the basis of pure time this seems fair for maturing a program and have expectations of success. There is a danger that may nullify it all. It can take three years to be able to recruit a really good crop of players. Before that the players may be willing, but not yet ready. By the time they are ready and able the losses may have piled up to the point that they aren't willing. There is a loss of confidence that thwarts success.

***

From personal experience I took over a situation that was very much down. The fall of the third year we had finally made in-roads and recruited a good group. As sophomores they played a lot. They were willing, going to be able, but certainly not ready. I was fired, a new coach came in and when those sophs were seniors they went to a bowl game. For a few years after I felt sorry for myself, fantasizing I would have taken them to the bowl game, they were my recruits. I now wonder if we would have? We had lost so many games that we, coaches and players, may not have ever been able to overcome the residue the losses had deposited.

***

In putting your coaching staff together, you want aggressive, energetic, ambitious people and the head coach should help them achieve their goals and move forward in their profession. If they are not loyal. . .dismiss them. Now understand, I say it easier than I ever executed it. Maybe I wasn't ruthless enough, I always worried about their families and what dismissal would do to their coaching careers. It is a great mistake. As Harvey Mackay says in his book, *"Swim with the Sharks,"* "it isn't the people you fire who make your life miserable, it's the people you don't."

***

It seems, and not based on scientific study, that the team that jumps all over each other prior to the kick-off gets beat more than they win. Maybe they lack confidence and are trying to create it.

***

There are two general kinds of football errors. There is the physical error and the error of discipline; the coach has more control over the latter. Piling on, off-sides, etc., can be controlled to a great degree. The better the athletic ability of the athlete, the fewer the physical errors.

***

Winners and losers have enemies. For the losers, the enemies may be termed "vigilante." They are made up of alumni, faculty, booster, team members. . .in other words those from inside your family. For the winners the enemies are more like assassins. There will be a few from within who believe the athletic success detracts from the image and mission of the institution. . .or are just plain jealous. For the most part, the assassins will be comprised of your opponents who have unsuccessfully competed against you. The assassins are more of an external group. Their goal is to "cut you down". . .the vigilantes want to "cut you up."

***

A single safety is effective versus a good punter. The punter that puts the ball high and it turns over can be fielded by a single safety, but the single safety is at the mercy of the line driver who can aim the ball to his left and right.

***

Rooming on the road deserves some consideration and through the years we have done it various ways, each serving a purpose at the time, but certain things can be achieved in the rooming scenario. To avoid any false perceptions and to have it strictly a clinical distribution, pair the players up in alphabetical order as they appear on the travel roster.

***

For a long time we paired up by positions, offensive guards together, fullbacks, etc. Our reasoning was that these youngsters could support each other in game preparation and reviewing assignments. This seems to have merit on paper, but I am not sure it served that purpose.

***

With the separation caused by platoon football, the real condition of the offense and defense not knowing each other very well, and to reduce the conditions that have one side of the ball thinking the other isn't doing their part, we made sure we roomed an offensive player with a defensive player, assisting them in knowing and supporting each other. This wasn't conducive to as organized a structure on the road, but it did break down barriers.

***

Beware of part-time coaches. Not those who work elsewhere, but are available for practice, rather those who want to play at coaching or like the title. They are there and not there. You can't count on them in your organizational structure and as a result you can't utilize them. They can't contribute and as a result aren't respected by the players. Such coaches can erode dedication and purpose and by permitting it you are sending contrary messages to the players and your staff.

***

For years our playbook was somewhere between Frank Lloyd Wright and Pablo Picasso. It was a work of art! However, I don't think the players appreciated the artistry of our geometric abstractions nor devote any time to absorbing its content.

***

We switched to include some learning principles. Some learn best through sight; others by hearing and some through writing. The switch included a playbook full of blank sheets. In a meeting the coach would diagram and explain the play and the players would draw it up in the playbook. Sight, sound and writing put forth near simultaneously. Though this thwarted the staff's sense of aesthetics, we knew the players had at least a one-time exposure.

***

Being out of coaching, returning to it and leaving, I have contemplated what the lure of coaching might be. I am sure it is a bit different with each individual. Ego may play a part in it. The excitement of it; the uncertainty; and the power of it. . .all these may be factors, but if you consider the way one lives, the rhythm of life and nature, there may be a correlation. In nature there is generally four seasons, with an annual rejuvenation and new beginning. Coaching allows a fresh start each year, new and unknown horizons. Last year's losers may be next year's world champions.

***

As a coach the rhythm of life ebbs and flows, but there is always the regeneration of the new season, the fresh start. Coaching is a conspicuous manifestation of human nature, the adventure into an unknown tomorrow with faith and hope.

***

We emphasized to players entering our program they entered with our respect. They didn't have to earn it. However, by their conduct, what was given could be withdrawn.

***

Having reached an age where most of my prayers are for thanks, I admit I still lobby for a few "gimmies."

***

It was declared illegal to bar a female reporter from entering the lockeroom as soon as the game was over. We were playing at Maryland the Saturday after the court decision. The game ended and as we entered the lockeroom, right behind a female reporter. I asked her not to enter. Both firm and polite, she insisted. I resisted. She told me she was raised with three brothers and would not be shocked or embarrassed. Good! I informed her if she took her clothes off she could go on in. She rejected the accommodation.

***

Truthfully, my concern wasn't the woman. This was twenty-five years ago and I truly feared her entering the lockeroom would shock and embarrass some of the youngsters on the team.

***

Had a player one time who was obviously a disturbed person. Erratic, violent, paranoid…he just couldn't remain on the team. I talked to him about taking a season off and getting some help. That threw him into a rage. I separated him from the team and managed a psychological evaluation. The psychiatrist reported the kid was "homicidal and suicidal." I asked but one thing from the doctor, could he reverse the order of the diagnosis?

***

Through the years I attended many, many conventions of the America Football Coaches Association, about forty years worth. Through the years the image has changed. I used to marvel at the camaraderie of the group. Long time coaches, long time rivals and long time friends. Many of the coaches would wear a coat and tie, but would wear their coaching shoes. Now, the shoe is no longer a coaching badge, everybody wears them.

***

Now, along with the coaching shoes, there are running suits, running shoes and styled haircuts. Very much a corporate image. At the last convention there was a guy in his running outfit riding up and down on the elevator. I think that was his exercise . . . going up was the challenge.

***

For me, sort of a sad evolution is the scarcity of the "big time" coaches being visible. When I was a young coach at the convention it was a thrill to see a Woody Hayes, Bobby Dodd, Bear Bryant, Rip Engle, Bill Murray, or even Amos Alonzo Stagg strolling though the lobby or having a cup of coffee. Not always accessible, but there! Not much of that anymore. Now most of the football coaching headliners that do attend the convention appear to enjoy their celebrity status as recluses, in their suites and only associating with each other. Too bad!

***

In 1958, the captain of the Pomona College football team was a young man named Ward Jones. He went on to earn his degree and during the Viet Nam war was a combat surgeon with the 101st Airborne. In Viet Nam, during a fire fight, he jumped out of a helicopter without authorization, under fire, to aid those in battle. He received the Bronze Star, Silver Star and many other honors for his actions. Ward believed football taught him courage, teamwork and loyalty to his comrades. I am not sure that is correct. I am more inclined to believe he brought those qualities to football, and his career.

***

In coaching Ward, I remember him as emotional, idealistic, intense and hard working. He was an over-achiever. A 100% team guy. Interestingly, one of his team-mates and good friend was a songwriter, performer and movie actor Kris Kristofferson. Kris played football, rugby, was a Golden Gloves boxer, Rhodes Scholar and on his way in a military career, having completed Ranger school and a helicopter pilot before heeding his own creative and artistic drummer and moved into the arts.

***

It strikes me, as quite possible the Good Lord is the CEO of the universe and may have turned the earth over to others. Mother Nature may be the force running the earth. With finite resources, global warming, deforestation and geometrically expanding population, it may no longer be "Mother" nature . . . just nature. The nurturing we associate with motherhood is being used up. I don't believe this will render the earth as barren as long as humankind has imagination and intelligence. Those two qualities will continue to provide solutions . . . It is called ingenuity.

***

I have always tried to live by an ethical and moral honor code, and generally I have conformed . . . however, as I have grown older and contemplate a number of things, it may not have been the courage to so live, rather, it may be I lacked the courage not to live by this self-imposed code.

***

Through the years I have been asked on numerous occasions to speak to various groups and organizations with the central theme being motivation. I enjoyed doing them and to this day I enjoy hearing them . . . they provide entertainment and can incite enthusiasm. However, I doubt they are of any lasting value.

Each will derive sustained motivation and enthusiasm from the dictates of one's own personality and psyche. Motivational speeches can be a tonic but not a panacea.

***

It seems we never forget when thought we got less than we deserved and never remember when have received more.

***

Before the days of player agent certification, agents and some pro scouts without scruples were a true pain in the side of the coach. No matter how much you lectured kids and made every effort to have them understand the severe sanctions if a player with eligibility remaining negotiated with an agent you never really knew, as the Kris Kristofferson song goes, what "silver tongued devil" was trying to seduce players.

***

Some pro scouts, with out the knowledge of their employers or the college coach would sneak in try to test players at an unauthorized time. In one incident at Utah State we had a youngster who was a fine football player and an outstanding basketball player. In March, in wintry Logan, Utah he sneaked the kid outside and timed him in the forty-yard dash. It was two days before the basketball team was heading to the NCAA tournament. What would have happened if the kid pulled a muscle sprinting in the cold?

***

As for the kid, in 1971 and 1972 the youngster played in both the NFL and NBA. Pretty good athlete, eh?

***

Among the most perplexing issues for the coach, athletics department and institution to address is that of the players running afoul of the law. The institution usually has a policy with a lower threshold than the athletic entity. One must be fair to all parties and the athlete must be afforded due process.

***

Our general guidelines within football allowed a player involved in a misdemeanor to participate until the matter was adjudicated; any action to discipline the player awaited the outcome. A felony allegation with preliminary facts to support it meant suspension from the team until adjudicated.

***

Be sure to comply with due process! The coach can't be as autocratic as he once was. Beginning primarily in the 70's and 80's, lawsuits became rather common in our society, coaches and institutions weren't any less targets of this proliferation.

***

Most of us have come to terms we are not immortal, but we are eternal. I believe there is an eternal life, though I must admit the logic of it escapes me. So, in the place of logic we have faith. There are people beyond counting have devoted their lives to serve and help others. We all know of Mother Teresa . . . all kinds, male and female, clerics and not, doing good works as she did. Most are little known; certainly their good works should entitle them to an eternal life. "Keep the faith!"

***

The Third Down

Certainly a great degree of athletic success depends upon the quality of the athletes involved. That aside, the glue and continuity of a program is the coaching staff. Technical knowledge and the ability to communicate it isn't of any value if the coach is disruptive to the staff and program.

***

Be careful whom you hire. Through many years of coaching, my criteria for staff was to hire "good people", the "good" not being directly related to football expertise. I have been in situations, however, where this requirement couldn't be the primary priority. There are people I have employed, always believing they would help the program, but on occasion it has been to assist a coach who needed a new opportunity. On occasion I have brought vipers into the fold, men who have lacked loyalty and support and who undermined me with staff and players. What is interesting is that in no situation I can recall has the viper gained. He may have damaged me, but he has not gained for himself.

***

Don't tolerate the viper. I have and I have paid for it. On one occasion I hired a coach unwanted by most because of age and with a reputation of one who disrupts staffs. He was a long-time acquaintance and I knew his reputation as a malcontent, but I thought he was old enough to have outgrown that phase. I knew football-wise he would contribute to the program and in return I could provide him with a needed feeling of self-worth and continued contribution. I was wrong. . .time hadn't tempered the viper. I learned this lesson too late in my career to recoup. Beware the viper!

***

Careful dealing with the fanatic. In armed terrorist activity the carnage among the innocent isn't a cause for remorse, rather it is jubilation for the havoc. However, in less violent environs the same attitude prevails. In that arena it is reputation and livelihoods destroyed maybe by fact or maybe by allegation. (That dirty word again).

***

Canceling the scholarship of a proven player can have impact with people quite removed from the player involved. My driving habits became more cautious when the "Vatican U." pulled St. Christopher's scholarship.

***

Having watched various teams practice, it seems many valuable practice minutes are lost in conducting drills that don't serve the skills required for that position. There are certain basic drills that serve all, but there is a point where drill time should be devoted to the needs of execution.

***

The offensive line is a good example. Often time is spent having all the offensive linemen work on pulling, yet two or three positions may never pull in the offensive scheme. Beyond the fundamental conditioning and agility drills, it is worth the coach's time to chart the most common defensive alignments to be seen, break down the assignment and techniques for each position of the basic offense, then conduct drills that serve the techniques required.

***

So many coaches, regardless of the harsh realities of the profession, are motivated in significant part by altruistic intentions. There are coaches who will never risk having a questionable citizen as a team member. There are others who recruit nothing else and this is often the result of a program asked to compete at a level that is not realistic. In these programs the coach may have to recruit individuals who are good football players, however, they are not very "good people." In order to compete against the colleges with the "good people" and the good players, they are in a position to attract only half the formula.

***

A team made up of marginal citizens will usually have problems. There isn't the positive group available to set the right direction. A few of the marginals in a program not only can be tolerated, but changed. Through their desire to compete, redirection in academic and social matters can be engineered.

***

There will be times when the coach will fail in this resurrection, and fan and media reaction can make it sound as though the team is made up of criminals and the coaches exercise no control. This will happen and is hard to accept, and though it may be just one or two out of one hundred, the generalization is made. The good kids and their accomplishments are ignored and the "shaky" kids saved aren't known. For the few saved, however, it is worth it. Yes, it is a pompous, arrogant attitude possibly on the part of the coach, yet if in the end through football, a productive citizen goes forth, what difference does the possible egocentricity of the coach make?

***

To have good team morale from within the group, players must know their roles and accept them. Without this, discontent can affect the team's play. Every team has some players who are just satisfied to be a part of the group. In most cases they aren't good enough to play and know it. There are some who would be terrified if they were called into action. There is a second group who think they should be playing, but there is no error being made by not doing so. Except for a few friends who will humor them, they offer no threat to the team and are essentially ignored.

***

The group that must be dealt with are those who are good enough to play, but aren't quite good enough to be starters. These are the role players who must sublimate their frustration for the good of the team. These players must understand that they may be good enough to play, but is there any reason the player ahead of them should be removed from the lineup?

***

There are some schools who must make big money on football and basketball to support other sports in their programs. For many, however, it is a matter of the high visibility and prestige that success brings, and with it the money required to keep the circle of needing money to maintain the program to keep the prestige.

***

There are a few teams who occupy the throne and in cycles will have their turn as king. However, most are pretenders to the throne with programs that want to be in the king's chambers, and these are the ones who are most suspect in cutting corners and breaking rules. They are in the chase, but not the hunt.

***

At times coaches overestimate the football playing reality of those young men who are very bright. At the prestigious institutions, where no admissions concessions are made for football players and the environment is one of scholastic pressure, coaches are often excited about the players' intelligence and how much and how quickly they can learn, but it is quite possible this doesn't transfer to performance. Often in such institutions the players' priorities are quite different. Their periods of football concentration may be only during football and all the knowledge imparted just creates another academic exercise that dulls enthusiasm and creates mental fatigue which is much more difficult to bounce back from than physical fatigue.

***

In coaching, it seems the older one gets or the longer one is in it the more daring his thoughts about the game, but the more traditional and staid he becomes in his style of play.

***

Over the past years it appears many offensive coaches have neglected experimentation with line-splits. Defensive coaches seldom work with their troops on how to react and play versus wider than normal offensive line-splits.

***

Non-scholarship football programs attract some very good football players. . . not as many as the scholarship programs, but still some pretty good ones. The scholarship programs are able to recruit the players they need to make their offensive or defensive strategy work. The non-scholarship coach must stay alert to make adjustments from what he would like to do to what best suits the skills of his players, and often this critical aspect is ignored.

***

An observation made through the years that may be difficult to take advantage of except in one way is that every QB under center, from high school through the pros, will drop his eyes at the instant of the snap. The only way I could ascertain to take advantage of it without affecting other reading and reaction responsibilities was for inside LB's when they are blitzing

***

Along this same line, the best read for down linemen and backers to react to offensive movement is the offensive linemen's hands. The hand will be the very first part of the body to move. The offensive lineman is as active as a statue until the hand moves. And the defensive people can be trained to read this movement through their peripheral vision, seeing it at the same time their concentration of vision is elsewhere.

***

If a coach is fired it is important that he limit himself to a short period of time for anger and self-pity. It is best to formulate a plan that positions one to pursue another job. If sure he wants to continue coaching, he needs to determine the limitations, if any, location places on the pursuit; inventory contacts and inquire about any vacancies of which they may be aware. December and January there are a lot of openings, but a lot of applicants as well. May, June and mid-August additional openings arise; not too many, but not many applicants, either.

***

Realize in spite of all the contacts a coach may have, very few will lead the way in helping. This is disappointing. The contacts may support the effort, but the coach had better locate the leads himself. A former head coach has a tough time landing even an assistant's job. Too often he is regarded as a threat. There will be occasions where the coach seeking a job will be told by administrators that they know he is capable of doing the job and that he would be a good choice, but the institution couldn't defend the decision with the public since the coach has been fired for losing.

***

Coaching is a profession where you don't get a return from the direct result of your effort. It goes through kids, who are all different, playing against a team trying to destroy what you have been working to do. Beyond this, you are then affected by the weather, referees and injuries.

***

Coaching isn't like selling. That is competition in personality and comparisons. Football is a direct, physical and violent encounter.

***

You are in a profession in which being fired is considered normal and acceptable conduct. When fired you feel betrayed. You feel diminished as a person. Why? Because you may have done a great job, but one injury to one player can mean defeat and dismissal. You don't deserve to be fired based on competence and effort.

***

Firing coaches is a carryover from human sacrifices to pagan gods, not only pagans, but burning the witches. . .in this case the coach is a warlock.

***

The latest term in what seems an Orwellian system of management is now referred to as the management of human resources. It seems to be another step in dehumanization. We are reducing the human condition to one of commodity, an inanimate object to be treated as a commodity or resource to be discarded like a desk or chair.

***

When minority coaches began to break the barrier and were hired on the staffs of what had been traditionally all white staffs, many of the coaches made the mistake of hiring the minority as an avenue to recruit minority kids or to serve as a role model for minority kids on the team. That was an error. You hired the minority coach for two reasons, at least I did. One, to coach and recruit as any other coach on the staff with a responsibility and a territory. The second reason was less sophisticated; it was to create opportunities for a group of coaches who had been denied for no professional reason.

***

If a coach is hired to deal with minorities, he is defeated before he starts. He won't have the respect of the very people he is supposed to be mentoring.

***

If the minority coach was to be a role model, it wouldn't be with the athletes on your team. They are already in college and you hope the best is made of it. The role should be for the younger kids who haven't started college, those who still have a future to pursue. And the model should be no more than a signal that opportunity does exist. It may not be as much as it should be. . .and will be. . .but it isn't hopeless. That is the only role model to have.

***

I am proud to be among the first to hire minority coaches, but what I wanted was a good coach who was also "good people," the same as others hired on the staff.

***

It's fun going to football clinics. Next time you go, look around and see how many coaches wear their coaching shoes to a clinic. Sometimes you'll see them in coat and tie and their coaching shoes. It is their badge, but with the latest styles this "badge of recognition" has been eroded; everybody wears athletic shoes.

***

Football is certainly a mental game and much of it because the coaches make it so. Recognizing formations and schemes require a certain amount of deduction and must be repeated enough in practice to become a reaction. The moral of the story. . . football must be played by reaction and not by deduction.

***

Tradition is a strong recruiting attraction. The present player wants to be part of a glorious "what has been." It can motivate the player. For the tradition to live the current player must contribute to it. The tradition excites the players psyche; his skills must keep it alive.

***

Through the years I noticed the young children of some staff members avoided me; ran from me or snarled. I have a pretty good idea of what their daddy had to say around the dinner table.

***

Football coaching is a demanding mistress. The relationship between coach and football is without sex but certainly not without passion. Often the coach's family is under a great strain and can easily feel deserted. Not only being physically deserted. . .but mentally as well.

***

At the beginning of fall practice a letter was written to each spouse. It acknowledged the pressures placed on the family because of football and I was cognizant of this and as best as I could, I would adjust so the coach could have more time at home. Over the years I have been surprised at the positive reaction this letter promoted.

***

The very successful programs; such as Penn State, Florida State, Nebraska and others have one thing in common. They have continuity of coaching staffs. That is not the common denominator of all successful programs. . .but it is of dynasties. So, does continuity bring success or success continuity? If given time the former will pay off. . .if given the reality the latter is more likely.

***

Different words have different meanings to different folks. There are three words that ignite a certain reaction in me. They represent for me the most useless word, the most vicious word and the most beautiful word.

***

<u>Potential</u> to me is the useless one. Potential teases and ignites hope, but in essence potential does nothing. If you execute the potential then it is no longer potential, but rather becomes fact. Until that time it lies there, looks at you and does nothing. The most vicious of words is <u>alleged</u>. It is a word for the gossip mongers and protects from slander and libel when slander and libel are the intent. It creates perceptions, and perceptions are deadly. The word <u>compassion</u> is the most beautiful and maybe the noun closest to God's heart.

***

Empathy and sympathy can also mean sorry for you, but rather you than me; love can be a selfish word. . .a word with strings on it. But compassion is a pure emotion. It has no meaning, nor motive, other than itself.

***

As a head coach or leader of any group one should honestly evaluate one's own strengths and weaknesses and then hire to compensate for the deficiencies.

***

It takes a lot of thought and planning, but platoon football with a staff sufficient for one-way football only requires overlapping of practice. Segments of the team, offense or defense, open practice and the other at the close of practice. In the middle both offense and defense work at the same time for skelly work and inside-outside drills. It isn't the best of coaching worlds, but it does allow segments of practice to have all coaches working with the offense and defense.

***

Post-practice conditioning need not always be running and sprints. Offensive linemen can assume their blocking position against the seven man sled. On the starting count they exert all out effort for five seconds. Take a five second break and repeat with enough resistance on the sled to keep it from moving. This is a great conditioner that simulates game effort and release. The danger is someone faking his effort.

***

The pooch kick; that short, high punt you hope won't go beyond the goal line. A punt of twenty to twenty-five yards. It is best not to have your regular punter do it as it can interrupt his rhythm. We have also done it with our field goal kicker doing the punting from the field goal formation. To avoid the ball rolling forward, we have the kicker hold the ball sideways, that is, with the points facing the sidelines.

***

A few years ago, in a doctoral dissertation, it was concluded that practice injuries didn't increase if there were no pre-practice calisthenics.

***

One year I had a 9-2 team that got it in their heads that they didn't want to go out on the field for pre-game calisthenics and warm-ups; except for the kickers we followed that regimen. I don't know what that means, but it didn't detract from success.

***

On occasion we have organized practice with the individual and fundamental work coming as the last phase of practice. It makes good sense, but was so contrary to established tradition it was upsetting to staff and players. It was good because at that time we could adjust our fundamental work to fit the needs as defined by that day's practice. We may need to work on something we didn't anticipate, but practice execution indicated the need. It also ended practice with an active, positive session.

***

The coach who can arrange the transfer of fundamentals and techniques to the next phase of practice will have a great advantage. Too often during fundamental work the players will execute well. As soon as practice moves to half-line work or team work the fundamentals succumb to assignments and adjustments. The coach often lessens his concentration on basics as well, as his interest is being sure the players know what to do more than how they do it.

***

It is my contention one should live by the P/P Principle. Put simply, it means principle versus paycheck. If one is working for a boss who violates what you believe in to the point it can't be tolerated, then quit. However, if the paycheck is a must and you can't afford to quit, then do your job.

***

There are all kinds of statistics we use to determine the success of a team, but the most meaningful is how many times a team takes possession on the opponent's half of the field.

***

After a turnover, players from the offense and the defense frantically sprint on the field in a state of anticipation or depression. It is beneficial to take a few seconds to have the entire group gather with the coach before going on to the field. This reduces the chance of having emotion rule order under such circumstances.

***

A way to put a bit of pressure on the defense is to not huddle on the first down after a ball exchange and on punts. Preparation for these two situations can be done on the sidelines.

***

Be aware that defensive linemen may get out of shape by mid-season. Full scrimmages are usually minimal and the defensive line runs a few steps and then holds up. About mid-season they need extra running. Offensive backs and linebackers, like running backs and wide receivers, get enough running. In fact, maybe too much if they must sprint after practice as well.

***

It seems the amount of time spent on punt returns and the amount of time other players stand around as this phase of the game is honed, would be time better spent in forgetting the return and just going for the block. Going for the block places tremendous pressure on the snapper and the punter as well as forcing the line to wait longer to release in order to protect the punter. The pressure can lead to bad punts as well as potential blocks. You will block more punts than get long returns.

***

It pays off to play a lot of kids during a game. This is so not just for the sake of their morale, but also because it means that every season you begin with players who have had game experience. You may begin the season with "unknowns," but not with the uninitiated.

***

Football coaches fall into four dominant categories, and though all coaches will have some of the traits of each, one category will dominate. First is the strategist, who is most intrigued by outsmarting the competition in the plays called and creating mis-matches. Next is the executionist, the coach who demands the play be run in a precise, correct manner. These types are the coaches who may be primarily fundamentalists and execution is a part of it. The next in line is the humanist. This coach is concerned with the human element. He enjoys the athletes and his relationship with them. The human equation is the most important. The final is the architect, the coach who is intrigued with building an organization and a program. Again, all coaches are in part practitioners of all types, but one will be the dominant interest.

***

Team meetings over forty-five minutes have diminishing returns. Players lose their attention and are only concerned when the meeting will end.

***

It seems grading players' performances can get very complicated. The elaborate systems lead to subjectivity and differences of opinion with the players. We graded on a one or zero system. The player was either successful in his execution or not. If not done properly, that becomes a verbal coaching point, but the player isn't downgraded.

***

When viewing the game tapes with the team we ask each player to have a sheet of notebook paper and grade himself on each play, ascertain his average then turn it in after the viewing. It is informative to see how he grades himself as compared to the coach. If there is a great difference then a discussion is in order. We also ask all players who play that position to grade the film. In this way they all observe, learn, and stay interested in the film review. . .in other words it discourages napping.

***

Formal calisthenics prior to practice were kept at a minimum. Very limited stretching, neck bridges and jumping-jacks for togetherness were about all that were done. After the preliminaries we used stations, with groups rotating from station to station. Each station involved fundamentals and movement. In this way the players warmed up well and worked daily on fundamentals of the game. In the early season each station was ninety seconds and later in the season the station was reduced to fifty seconds. Early there was a fifteen second break between stations, reduced to ten seconds as the season went on.

***

Mental fatigue has always been more of a worry than physical fatigue. Physical fatigue can be addressed by a change in the routine and reducing the level of physical activity. Mental fatigue carries over and builds. A change in the routine can help. The players need to be refreshed and their interest renewed. Mental fatigue leads to a lack of concentration and focus. Something as simple as using the swimming pool for conditioning or swimming instead of jogging the day after a game helps. Only imagination limits avenues to reduce the ramifications of mental weariness.

***

The lost day. Often when a team is given a day off unexpectedly to "refresh" them, the next practice is a lost one. It seems the players are sluggish and out of synch.

***

Practices need to be designed to encompass two conditions: intensity and concentration. They need not be simultaneous, but they must be included in the scheme. The closer to game day the more important concentration becomes. Our pre-practice routine included concentration in the stretching and intensity in the stations.

***

Where it can be done, usually only the first game or two, it is a good idea to conduct practice at the same time you will play the game. It establishes a rhythm that is not all out of whack on game day.

***

In post-practice sprints we tried to sprint with more game-like reactions. Twenty yard sprints, come back quickly, form a huddle for break, and then up and sprint again. We also sprinted thirties and forties, but never over forty. Beyond that distance linemen and backers tend to lose their form and begin reaching in their stride and chance pulling a muscle.

***

In post-practice sprints it is beneficial to have the players remove their pads. Studies have been conducted showing that players sprinting without pads develop a more efficient running form than those wearing pads, and when pads were used those sprinting without them did not lose speed because they retain good running technique.

***

On occasion experience can defeat talent, but as a steady diet it will lead to anemia. The best diet is talent and the best way to develop it is through experience.

***

A rule of thumb, if your ball carrier shows you the back of his jersey, block nothing, you're better off cheering.

***

Line blocking in setting up the screen requires considerable technique and finesse. A change to the standard method is for the offensive lineman to execute a cut block at the feet of the rusher. The rusher will jump over the man and really go for penetration.

***

Practicing the techniques of the drive block by blocking down a board is common. An alternative is to use strips of carpet rather than boards. The end result is the same without the danger of turning an ankle on the board.

***

For a right handed passer, to avoid throwing across the body, on rolling left, turn up field before passing. If the passer turns up field then there is no right or left.

***

Your coaching staff had better like each other and respect the head coach. Negative attitudes are sensed by the players and these attitudes will divide the team within hours.

***

If the head coach needs to coach a phase of the game it is best it be the kicking game. In this way he can have his choice of personnel without creating the potential problem of cheating the other side of the ball one way or another if he coaches with the offense or defense.

***

The larger a bureaucracy gets, the harder it is to admit a mistake and the more reluctant to rectify it.

***

On a wide play away from the tight end, the backside or tight end and tackle can double team the defensive tackle. Those two aren't going to do too much downfield, but with the double team they do a couple of things; they can break defensive keys and physically wear down the defensive tackle and that might prove to be vital late in the game. They also get some practice on the double team under game conditions.

***

Conventional wisdom and good coaching are often demonstrated by the ball carrier while running in the open field and switching the ball to the outside arm or away from the pressure. That's good coaching and good play. . .except that when the ball is being switched, it seems there is a good chance of it being fumbled. It may be best to just drill the ball carrier to protect the ball and forget about switching.

***

Whenever I read the waiver wires in the press about professional players being cut I always regard it as the epitaph of dreams.

***

With a good team you can not always be sure they have played to the best of their ability. It is easier to judge if a poor team has played as well as it could.

***

The ultimate pass rush ends in a sack, but it isn't the only measure of a successful rush. Also successful is the rush that puts the passer out of rhythm, and that happens primarily by forcing the passer to release the ball without stepping into the throw.

***

Often one's empathy for another is sincere, but the underlying factor may be guilt or gratitude. It can be a combination of both, depending on the glass "being half full or half empty."

***

It is human spirit that fuels hope.

***

Colleges with super academic reputations achieve this status by the students they attract. It is the students who make a school top academically. . .not the reverse.

***

A measure of a mature educational institution is having the confidence to pursue athletic success and not cringe from it nor be embarrassed by it, or regard it as a threat to the institution's quality.

***

"Won't do" is a mental decision. . "can't do" may be a physical fact.

***

A fumble is often the result of a slight relaxation by the ball carrier as he hits the ground and allows the belly of the ball to hit the ground as the ball carrier does. It literally bounces out of the crook of the arm.

***

Two big "B's" in football--on offense no bad plays and on defense no big plays.

***

When a player is injured and down on the field, the head coach should go on the field for all injuries or for none. If he only goes on occasion, then when he does go it creates anxiety on the part of the player and the fans.

***

An often neglected coaching point for the receiver, and yet one that can really improve receptions, is to constantly emphasize to the receivers to get their shoulders around. We often talk about the head, but include the shoulders as well.

***

Touch and when to release are two vital factors for a good passer. Some have the tools, but delay in releasing the ball. A simple drill is to put three receivers or more downfield holding an arm pad. The coach stands behind the passer and, as the passer sets up, points at a receiver who then drops the pad and that is whom the QB throws to. It helps in anticipation.

***

Both good and bad things can happen when a chance is taken. Enough good must happen not to discourage taking a chance in the future, but even taking a chance requires some preparation for the possibility of success.

***

A few years ago we played a game in post-season play against a team playing a college 43 defense. One where the guards were covered and the linebackers off the offensive tackles. This was at a time when most everybody was running a 52 defense. We were a straight ahead blocking team and hadn't faced a 43 all year. The basic challenge was our guards playing with a big, strong player on the line across from them and our tackles blocking linebackers who were off the ball and could run.

***

With less than a full week to practice, the teaching challenge was to get the guards and tackles able to execute primarily each other's technique. It dawned on me an easier adjustment would be to switch our guards and tackles on the line. It required the players to line up in a different place but they could execute what they were used to doing. It worked and we won.

***

Most coaches are emotionally attached to those who play for them. When a youngster has problems, the coach wants to assist even though the rules prohibit it. It is helpful if, at the beginning of each season, the team is told not to come to a coach asking for a loan or some other material benefit. Tell the team it is against the rules and to do so would mean the coach's job would be placed in jeopardy. I have found this most helpful in avoiding very uncomfortable situations.

***

With all the television revenue available and the concern of what to do with it, consideration should be given to establishing a loan fund made available to athletes. It could be confined to family emergency type situations.

***

The rule that denies a scholarship athlete from working in the off-season is a stupid one. At its inception it made philosophical sense, but in practical terms it is as discriminatory as any rule could be. It would be easy to establish a system to avoid abuse. The married player really suffers. The inability to work causes a financial hardship on the family and could threaten the marriage itself. If the wife can't work then there are real problems. Our rule of thumb was to tell the athlete his scholarship check would cover rent and utilities. . .the wife's employment would have to do the rest.

***

The single factor that can dictate a game is speed. Speed on the offense can make the big play anytime and can intimidate the defense. More importantly, however, is what speed does for the defense, and one thing it can do for the defense is to make up for error.

***

Visions and dreams are attainable and fantasies are for another world. As goals are pursued, be able to distinguish the difference between the two.

***

Don't neglect to instruct the team on when a kick or fumble can be advanced. Tremendous opportunities to turn games around are taken away because players don't know the rules.

***

In 1988 the University of Miami in Florida hired a number of students to secretly monitor athletes' attendance in class and report to the athletic department if they didn't attend. It seems athletics has paved the way again in implementing Orwellian standards.

***

It would be good training for all the football players to work in the off-season with a sprinting coach, not just to improve speed or running form, but rather something more fundamental to football. It would train the players to come out of their stance low and with force. Too many players stay low a step and then raise up.

***

Every organization has a power base. In football the bases are the staff, the players, the faculty, alumni and friends, and possibly the media. Each leader, the coach or the athletic director, have a constituency that is their power base. It is these power bases that provide political support when a conflict develops. In the scheme of things it seems the athletic director's power base is a more reliable source than the base the coach develops. The coach, as a primary entertainer, has a more fickle base of power.

***

Integrity and truth should be a matter of ethics; however, there may be a practical aspect as well. . .it is called memory. If one lies there is the aspect of not remembering what lie was told to whom, so memory, for some, may dictate an illusion of integrity.

***

A fickle business this coaching. . .a coach can do a great job of coaching, but not win and be fired. He can do a great job of coaching and win. . .and still get fired. The reason is the high visibility and celebrity status a coach can have, even if just locally. There are all kinds of people with influence who, for whatever reason, can become the assassin of the coach's career.

Remember the coach at Pitt a short time ago who had a lifetime contract that was terminated eight months later?

***

On a personal basis I have been hired and did a good enough job to be hired for what appeared to be a better job. I have been fired for losing and at one time the president of my college announced I had a "lifetime job." The president departed for a new position and within a year and a half the new president managed to let me know it was time to move on, even after taking the team to the playoffs for the first time in the school's history. The moral of the story: It is safer for your career to win rather than lose, but it isn't a safe-guard. You just don't know the agenda of those who can eliminate you. And I am sure it isn't just in coaching.

***

Too bad victories can't be placed in a bank and draw interest and then, in a down season, the interest can be expended. Recently, a coach who had been at a small college for twenty-seven years and had a .700 winning percentage moved into a conference that was too much for the school and after three mediocre seasons he was fired.

***

In spite of good contracts, there is a perverse justification to coaches jumping contracts. Regardless of the contract, without success the coach will be fired. Once fired, regardless of the dollars received in the separation, it is tough for the coach to ever coach again. By changing jobs at an opportune time, it is a fresh start and may add longevity to a coaching life.

***

What is wrong with collegiate athletics isn't athletics. It is the human dynamic and money. Athletics is the victim, not the perpetrator.

***

Providing a stipend to a player won't reduce illegal payments. Nor will it reduce the temptation; again, it is the human condition. To control the illegal inducements, action must be devised and executed to thwart the source.

***

No program will be successful without administrative support. And that support means resources, but as much as anything, the administration must not be ashamed of success and the pursuit of it. The situation will dictate success far more than the coach.

***

In athletics there is the overt measure of success; winning and losing. The reality, however, may not match the expectations and dreams. The coach is often discharged based on unfulfilled dreams and not on the reality of the situation.

***

It is interesting to observe how often, when plays are being sent in from the sidelines, that the messenger system never moves up and down the sideline. They will stay on the offensive side of the bench. The messenger system should move up and down the sideline, as close to the action as they can, and in this way the distance the messenger has to run is reduced and as a result time is conserved.

***

Stretching is very important in modern day athletics, but I must admit, in football I don't like it. Not because of the need, but because it seems to be a "downer." After pre-game and pre-practice stretching, intensity seems a notch lower, making it an ordeal to begin practice with any eagerness or enthusiasm. This happens not so much prior to a game because the adrenaline is pumping and the players are anxious, but it sure seems that way before practice.

***

We developed certain stretching routines to be done before the official start of practice. We have the players work at their positions, then for formalized exercise we do those that recapture a level closer to what is wanted in practice.

***

It would be ideal to never have a QB run a play at any stage of practice without a center exchange. This isn't always practical, so to compensate we have made all our QB's and wide receivers learn how to snap the ball. Not just to bring it up, but to snap and step. In this way the QB's can always be receiving a snap.

***

A way to get extra passing and receiving work is to have the off QB listen to the play in the practice huddle. Then go to the wide receiver away from the play and work a pattern with that wideout.

***

Young players or players lacking confidence tend to need the security of being close together. As splits isolate defenders, offensive linemen are isolated as well, and without confidence offensive linemen will hesitate to split out as required.

***

Coaching takes a hold on individuals that is never shed. After a few years in coaching, even if successful alternative employment takes place, the individual seems to regard himself as a coach first. The "calling" never leaves, and each day coaching is thought about.

***

The recent introduction of plastic visors to protect the eyes may serve another purpose, especially for quarterbacks wearing tinted ones. . .it deprives linebackers and defensive backs from "reading" the QB's eyes in the passing game.

***

When education and athletics are discussed in an adversarial atmosphere, though the ideal is philosophical, the actuality is quite different. It would seem reality was the first of the two to operate in the structure of man. It may be philosophy was the next logical step, either to justify reality or to alter it so there would be some semblance of order to the human condition. Philosophy can temper and influence reality but can't replace it.

***

Coaches can give great lectures on strategy and tactics that are irrefutable in the abstract. Where this breaks down is in the human equation. . .the players who must execute may lack the skills. That's a reality. That is why it is so very important that considerable coaching time be devoted to personnel in terms of skills and placement.

***

It seems practical to teach players getting up from the ground after a play to get up "fanny first." With aggressive, swarming defenses it would reduce the chance of injury because of a late hit or from another player being knocked into the pile. That part of the anatomy seems a bit more durable and able to absorb such blows.

***

Teams running the wishbone, who understand and execute it well but fail to have success, can usually be reduced to one consistent factor: they lack the speed to make the pitch a long-gain threat. The pitch man should be able to outrun the defense.

***

There is some validity to the idea that pure passing teams are unable to be "hard nosed" running teams when they need to be. A method for developing the aggressive style of play needed in the running game and doing it in the limited time a passing team can give the running game, is to run the wedge play. Not that this should be the running game, but it is a way to develop the mind-set a running game needs.

***

Just remember. . .be sure you have enough time to practice what you do.

***

Athletics, academics, finances, philosophy, livelihoods, and public pressures are all a part of the athletic equation. It's apples, oranges, bananas, peaches, pears and prunes. All are fruits, but all are different. The task of reformers is to create a compote. . .sugar-free of course.

***

The best offense is debatable, and to choose one and stick with it requires knowledge and confidence. A basic ingredient of running the "I" formation is its ability to permit a variety of attacks. The danger is doing a little bit of a lot of things, but not fully developing one.

***

On the other hand, a wishbone team or a run and shoot team must fully commit to that style of play. It requires dedication and courage because the "dye is cast." The advantage of a single tactic of attack is that it allows the full development of that attack; it is fully exploited.

***

When two run-and-shoot teams play, it is good advice to bring a sleeping bag and a picnic lunch, because it is going to be a long, long game.

***

If a program is unable to recruit the specific skills needed to run a specific offense, then the coaching staff had better be able to adjust and change the attack to meet the talents of the kids they have in the program.

***

The idea of having separate offenses within the same team has always been appealing. One set of backs and receivers who run a drop-back pass offense and another for the wishbone or veer. It really is simple to do for the backs, the problem that arises is that it is too much for the offensive line. They have only so much time to develop schemes and work them against various defenses week to week. The mental end of dual and triple offenses can be learned. . .there just isn't time enough to practice what is needed for competent execution.

***

The wishbone offense changes defensive strategies, and with that comes the pressure it exerts on the defense every play; not the physical pressure as much as the mental. Defensive players are assigned to individuals, it is a "man to man" defense versus the running game. Even when a defender sees another with the ball he must stay with his man. Pursuit is often neutralized, and if the defender's man gets the ball, then there is one on one pressure and a tackle can't be missed.

***

Dangers exist in coaching styles. The autocratic coach is one who dominates. There is danger this type of leadership will stifle other staff members, or inhibit and possibly intimidate them. It can keep good ideas suppressed. The delegator has a different concern. By allowing staff members to contribute, lead, and have authority, there is the possibility staff authority will break down and the assistants will assume the dominant roles and believe they can act indifferently, or unilaterally within the program. Coach according to your personality, but attempt to compensate for the pitfalls.

***

The devil made me do it. Maybe. Evil may create a scenario, but free will makes the decision.

***

The field of sports medicine is recent and exciting. Just be sure those who say they are "sport medicine" people are practitioners in the field and are not just excited by the glamorous sound of the title.

***

The pendulum often swings in the non-high-powered programs. If the team is a strong one there will be those who will want to reduce the success in the name of academics. After a few years of this, then the emphasis will swing back to success. The victim...the coach.

***

There is a unique cooperation between opposing teams. The offense tries to do certain things while the defense attempts to abort the offensive plans. The cooperation is in the recognition of rules limiting the conduct of these offensive and defensive plans. Without these rules of cooperation the game would be unbridled mayhem.

***

Should the classroom teacher be placed under the same gun as the athletic coach? Coaches recruit with the idea they will attract athletes who are talented enough to win contests. If they are not (in other words, the athletes fail to win). . .the coach is fired.

***

If the admissions director certifies that a student has the grades and ACT or SAT scores to be successful in college, then it should be the responsibility of the academic "coach" to be able to teach and prepare the student well enough so the student will pass the class. If enough fail to pass the class, then the "academic coach" should be placed in the same precarious situation as the "athletic coach."

***

Of course, there are always some marginal athletes attracted, who may or may not be talented enough to "pass" the athletic test. For the classroom coach there will be a few marginal students. The instructor should not have that student count against the instructor in the failure quotient.

***

Possibly a more meaningful measure of the quality of "academic coaching" would be to have a class in a subject compete against the class from another college. There could be rules for the contest such as the parameters of the questioning in the subject; there could be referees (judges) who are regarded as experts in their knowledge of the material. Maybe the chemistry team could have a full schedule. . .WPI, MIT, RPI...because of budget restrictions they may be unable to travel to Cal Tech or Colorado School of Mines, etc.

***

The above, obviously, is written with tongue in cheek, but you must regard the premise has a degree of logic to it, but I am not sure it is a truth. . .and I wouldn't try and defend it other than to make the correlation which does exist that binds education as a whole. The essential difference between academics and athletics is the forum. . .one is in the public's eye, the other less so.

***

The most captivating emotion of sport for the participant and spectator is the triumph of the human spirit. That moment of joy is often expressed in tears, when one has achieved the ultimate. The success is the symbol of work and effort.

***

Human spirit at its best is the Special Olympics, the purest of organized athletics.

***

"The upper class is a nation's past and its middle class its future. . ." so says writer Ayn Rynd. Though it seems that it is the lower class that provides the vehicle of the past and future.

***

The military is not a good example of democracy as we perceive it. It is, however, the repository with the mission to protect the institutions and practitioners of our democracy.

***

The searching for and acquiring of knowledge is not cost effective, but its application is.

***

The director of a group may lead by authority, but he is not necessarily a leader. A leader, by the force of this quality will direct, overtly or by attitude. Leadership requires certain principles, but there are intangible qualities as well. The reluctant leader may submerge these qualities, but they can't be drowned.

***

For most teams Sunday is a work-day, a change from the usual routine, but a day with football obligations. We had fine success by having supervised recreational swimming for our players after checking in with the trainer. It was supervised and included some lap swimming to stretch out, a little frolicking, but no real "horse play." Be sure a certified lifeguard or two are on duty.

***

It always amazed me how the players seemed to know everything before it was supposed to be known. How did they know? Often in ways never realized. Maybe they overheard a remark, maybe somebody in the know tipped them off. . . but they knew.

***

During the season on one or two occasions, when I thought the kids were getting bored or mentally fatigued I would not tell the players, but about a half hour or so into the practice I would cancel and send the kids in. It seemed they always knew. In spite of telling the coaches to keep it to themselves. . . the players knew. I reached the point where I told nobody. The coaches didn't know and still the gridders sensed it. How?

***

Years later I found out who the snitch was . . . me! In those days I smoked cigars and a practice was two cigars worth. On the short days I only had one cigar in my pocket and the kids picked up on it. One cigar meant, it's over early. I wonder if three cigars would have enraged them?

***

Full effort is a goal the coaching staff aspires to for each player. Assuming this is achieved, there is still a threshold of effort that permits the unbelievable play and that threshold is unending effort. It is the unending effort that makes the play that shouldn't be made.

***

When the good athlete is injured the impact is more than one of physical well-being. The athlete is threatened. It can be a threat to the very center of his being. A threat to the athlete's very core of self-worth and the fear of losing this essence compounds the injury well beyond the physical.

***

It would seem courage falls into three categories; the first would be instinctive or reactive courage, that of doing a courageous act when there isn't time to evaluate. It is a spontaneous reaction to a situation. Next would come the courage of will, performing an act that you fear, but you overcome the fear to perform the act. Finally would be the courage of commitment. To perform an act over a period of time that has dire consequences as a potential; to put yourself on the line for a principle.

***

Verbal leaders and motivators can achieve goals for the group, but verbal motivation is more the tool of the manipulative type leader. It is quite different than the leader by example or respect. Verbal motivation is easier to establish than other types, but more quickly dissipated if outcomes don't match words.

***

Verbal motivators need turnover of personnel to maintain motivation. Motivation by examples are enduring.

***

The leader of the group should attempt to cultivate the group, not control it. However, if cultivation doesn't work then control must be exercised and this may be difficult to do after the cultivation attempt. Control may have been lost during the enlightened leadership.

***

Defeat lowers self-esteem and thus diminishes ego. Success will do the opposite. At times, success may be for the individual but escape the group; both success and failure have psychological impact. Failure (or a continued lack of success) can bring antisocial behavior as compensation for lost esteem.

***

At times, when the legal system has finished with a criminal, it almost seems the crime has been legalized.

***

The purpose of audibles at the line must be defined. For us it wasn't to call the "big play" at the line, but rather to get out of the bad play. We wanted to avoid running a play into the strength of the defense.

***

If thought about, life is like a forced march; it ends at the end. Any respites or diversions in no way affect the march. Memories may divert one, but it is only a respite; the march is still forward. . .and relentless.

***

So much is commercial it is quite possible that Santa Claus has become a shill for the credit card industry.

***

There are mood swings among teams, and even the best of coaches really can't control these moods on a consistent basis. There are some games where the emotions tell the mind. "It's a big one and be excited." In most games the mind tells the emotions to be excited. . .the emotions don't always listen.

***

Autobiographies or biographies tell about the events in one's life. . .for the poet, the poetry reveals more about the essence of the life than the facts of it.

***

"Know thyself." The athlete who cares to learn through participation can learn to "know thyself" and others as well; to respect oneself and then to respect others, both team-mates and opponents. I have often thought this may be the most important and most subtle of what athletics has to offer.

***

Television is not the cause of corruption in athletics. At least not the corruption of athletes and boosters. That has existed from the beginning. It may be true, however, that television's big dollars have seduced institutions. In the past it was the prestige of the winner that drove the wheel of athletic corruption. For many major colleges it is the money that is fueling the motor. Individuals have corrupted athletes but television and the need for dollars has seduced institutions.

***

Young athletes are dreamers and are capable of dreams in many areas. As the coach, it is part of your responsibility to keep the dreams alive and, as the athlete grows and matures, the coach can help to fuse reality into the dream so that it turns into an attainable goal. Coach, help them to dream. Don't create a cynic. The conditions of life can do this to a less than confident, less than self-respecting person.

***

You can't do something without doing something and that "something" will be disagreeable to some or maybe all. "Nothing" is hollow, it isn't something. To do something. . <u>do something</u>!

***

When you are new on the job and offer a suggestion your colleagues agree with, they extol the advantage of the "new blood" you have brought; however, if it is something that is a threat. . .then you are a wise guy. "He's new. . .what does he know?" Remember, coach, your team is entertainment, but you are the entertainer. The act gets old.

***

Too often we assume a lack of intelligence when it is really a mask of ignorance.

***

"You question my integrity?" It seems the universal battle cry of the scoundrel when confronted.

***

We cheer the players, the coaches, and the overall production of the game. Without the trainers, equipment supervisors, publicity folks, and team managers it would be a different looking product. They are on the job seven days a week during the season.

***

And for games, the grounds crew gives an aesthetic quality that adds to the drama. The very boundaries of the game are created by them. Sometimes we may forget the role of the support people. . .or fail to appreciate or acknowledge them.

***

If a coach wants to know the true pulse of the team, talk to the trainers and equipment manager. They deal with the players at a level where the truth comes out. My experience has been that the trainer can head off many problems before they really blossom. The coach can not compromise the trainer in this role of trust that the trainer has with the players, but the trainer has a feel for what is happening that the coach doesn't.

***

If the population of the world was reduced to a village of 1000 people, sixty would be American; 800 would be non-white; 500 would go to bed hungry and without electricity or plumbing.

***

Coaches always implore their teams to concentrate. As a coach I thought it important that they concentrate on the right thing. To me there are two kinds of concentration. With the first, the assignments can be so complex that the concentration is keeping straight on what to do; the second is concentration on execution. The execution aspect has the most effect on performance. Consequently, I thought it important that we weren't so complex that our concentration was squandered in the "what" to do rather than the "how" to do.

***

As coaches we always preach the value of athletics and the lessons of life learned. We all say just about the same thing. . .but consciously or subconsciously, twenty years later what do you hope your players got out of athletics? I hoped for three things: integrity of actions, discipline for living, and respect for others. That is if I contributed at all through coaching.

***

Football coaching is a never ending set of tasks that must be done on a day to day basis. Day to day, week to week, month to month, and year to year. The axiom: it must be done and until it's done. . .it's not done.

***

Communism has collapsed. Communism, as practiced in the USSR, was to provide cradle to grave care and a job for life. It also bred complacency and dulled creativity and progress. Capitalism rewards creativity and progress. . .but it also whets greed and ruthlessness.

***

It has always been a source of concern to me when I see kids used as tools for one adult to get back at another. Coaches, teachers or whatever supervisory role an adult has over young people, don't tolerate any kid being used in this way.

***

Through the years, it seems to me we often honor some of the shady characters in the coaching profession.

***

There are so many coaches eager to move ahead in the profession that there is not much respect for coaches by those doing the hiring. A job opens and the applications for the post are in the scores.

***

When I was a young coach I would listen to the old coaches telling stories about their exploits and experiences. I promised myself I would never do that. Who cares? Well, years have passed and now I'm doing what I said I wouldn't. What I realize now is that I don't much care if the listener is interested or not. I'm not telling the stories for their enjoyment. . . it is for mine!

***

When the stock market goes down many investors sell their stocks to cut their losses. When a team is losing, the investors cut the coach.

***

To illustrate how precarious the football coaching profession is, in 1967 I was among twenty-one head coaches hired for their first head coaching job in Division I. After the 1977 season, a decade later, only one remained. (No! Not me.)

***

<u>It is unfortunate but true. . . too often when we treat one with kindness and consideration it is regarded as weakness.</u>

***

Two standard rules we had . . .only the head coach could dismiss a player from the team. . . and the head coach would not make the decision until the next day. By doing that we avoided emotional decisions and getting cornered by reaction and not decisions based on deliberate thought.

***

At one time we had a youngster who was a consistent player; was a pre-med student, married and just a great young man. Hard working and a real team guy. His wife worked as a fork lift operator to help him get through school. Each time our team traveled she would bake great cookies for the players to eat on the road.

***

One day he had a poor game and I got after him. I brought his play up again at Tuesday's practice. He walked off the field. Was that the end of him on the team? Should I drop him or had he quit? The next day he came to see me, apologized, and said he wanted to stay on the team. He agreed he had to be disciplined and would accept whatever that was. What should the punishment be? His punishment? The next time his wife made cookies . . .a dozen for me.

***

Here was a young man who was responsible, hard working . . . just a first-class person. With all kinds of pressures, me being on him was more than he could handle that day . . . so he removed himself from the situation. I would not have asked him back. . . but I wasn't going to grind him if he returned. The cookies were good.

***

We think of the Ten Commandments as rules of religion, maybe of a higher order than the human species can deal with on a day to day basis. A perspective for the Commandments in a more secular way may be the incorporation of Mahatma Gandhi's Seven Sins. They are: Wealth without Work; Pleasure without Conscience; Knowledge without Character; Commerce without Morality; Science without Humanity; Worship without Sacrifice and Politics without Principle.

***

As political correctness dominates a society becoming more hostile and violent and so many of us more and more remote from each other, I find myself unwilling to compliment one of the other gender as how it might be interpreted, by a fanatic looking for a cause for harassment, nor smile or wink or wave at a little kid. . . it may be regarded as perverted by some goof. It is safer to disengage.

***

Too often, worthy and legitimate causes are taken over by the lunatic fringe. Though a minority, they intimidate the majority. It is not uncommon for the fringe group to gain attention and authority beyond the cause's worth. What is sad, is that the majority tends to capitulate, feel invalidated by their leaders and withdraw from participation in the system, leaving it to the fringes who often become more oppressive then their perceived oppressors. I sometimes wonder if "political correctness" isn't the code for "societal hostility."

***

If athletics will exercise its role as a cooperative effort, where a variety of people come together to achieve a common goal with respect for self, team-mates and opponents. . then an oasis of balance remains.

***

Recently I was watching a post-season bowl game. The coach of one of the teams had been fired and this was his final game. Yet throughout the game the announcing team talked about the new coach; interviewed him during the game and asked present players what they thought of the new coach. Beyond tasteless, it seemed obscene to me. . . talk about bodies not being cold!

***

In a scholarship athletic program the walk-on athlete is at a great disadvantage. Just about every program will have a walk-on who made it and was awarded a scholarship. However, when the walk-on appears there is an assumption he isn't good enough to play or he would have been recruited by somebody. Then, when the youngster does show well, it isn't taken seriously; it is hard for the coaches to believe an unrecruited kid could be better than one they had recruited.

***

Coaches spend considerable time trying to assist problem players. Players with grade problems, citizenship problems, interaction problems. Often it fails, but just when the coach thinks it is all a waste, one youngster responds, and the coach is charged up and keeps on keepin' on.

***

A number of years ago the high school coaches in Philadelphia were concerned that they had good players who were not being recruited. They organized an all-star game to be played in the spring. I told them I would save one scholarship and if a player was good enough it would be awarded. It was given to a youngster. Our coaches were angry at me because the kid wasn't big enough to play; in spite of outstanding grades, the admissions office was livid because the SAT's were the lowest ever admitted. Result. . .the player was named All-American and was an all-league selection in the Canadian Football League for years. . . academically, he was on the Honor Roll seven of eight semesters.

***

Having served in the dual role of athletic director and football coach at a mid-size college for a number of years, it came home to me rather quickly that football suffered. There were issues that as the football coach I would have fought very hard to achieve. As the athletic director as well, I was more hesitant and didn't pursue some issues at all, my fear is that I would be perceived as using the dual post to provide football with an advantage.

***

It seems kids don't organize games anymore. When I was a youngster teams were made up of kids and by kids. No Little League or Pop Warner teams. In baseball I was the bottom guy on the team; I played right field unless it was a left-sided hitter, then I went to left field. But I played. Since adults now organize and supervise kid's games, I wonder who's playing right field?

***

Too many quarterbacks, throwing from the pocket, release the ball and then stand there and watch the result of the play. In colleges and the pros the standing quarterback has been nailed, and not infrequently received a late hit and had numerous injuries. After the passing action is completed, the QB should cover the pass. He knows exactly where the ball is going. We wanted him to keep an inside out angle in the event of an interception, using the sideline. If intercepted then the quarterback becomes the safety. Most of all, by covering, the QB is moving and getting away from the danger of being a standing target.

***

The increasing pressure on admissions directors to enroll students has seen a considerable increase in replacing them for failing the task. Athletics have always been a vital factor in attracting students. . .and many a coach has been dismissed because admissions rejected those key kids who would mean victory. I certainly hope, under this new pressure, admissions directors won't marginalize the admissions criteria just to have numbers to keep their jobs.

***

Seeing players taunt their opponents and even opposing coaches, certainly diminishes the thesis regarding respect for others. Much of the conduct, in certain neighborhoods, would be a real threat to continued living. In many ways it is closer to a gang fight than an athletic competition. Many teams with their between play shenanigans are making up for their lack of skill during the play. A coach who refuses to control such conduct is either unaware of his obligations as a coach or afraid of his players. Either way, football is the victim.

***

The erosion of civility in our society is clearly reflected in the way we play our games. Not just obnoxious players, but coaches as well, who denigrate opposing players and coaches by running up big scores. Maybe reading Toynbee regarding the collapse of civilization and its root causes should be required.

***

The coach often acts as though he should get the credit when the team has an outstanding student. The coach may encourage, support, and praise such an athlete. . .but the reality is that the youngster would be a good student with or without the team. Maybe we want to give athletics credit for its scholars because we always need to justify the "worth" of our life's work.

***

There are many football coaches who can package an unstoppable football scheme. Give them the chalk and the chalkboard and it would be impossible to lose. But neither the coach nor the chalk and chalkboard will play a down. The offense should be limited to those things the offensive line has the time to learn, repeat, and execute; for the defense the same holds true for the secondary and backers.

***

Football and athletics in general don't build character; what it does do is bring out character traits. If the athlete will be honest and look at himself he will discover how he reacts to adversity and success. He will know if he is a quitter, griper, hustler, persistent, loyal or whatever and, realizing his individual shortcomings, can discipline himself and modify his behavior.

***

Giving up competition, whatever the reason, is a trauma for most athletes. In football, it may be difficult to understand players' reluctance to stop playing when it means the end of bumps, bruises, injuries and general discomfort. It isn't the physical misery and mental pressure the athlete misses. . .it is the loss of the camaraderie among the team members, the special affection and understanding among those who have worked, sacrificed and at times suffered in pursuit of a common goal. This is what is missed and the void is never filled again. It is a unique human experience.

***

The coach must pay special attention to the player who is injured and lost to the team for weeks or a season or a career. If not corrected, the injured player often withdraws from the team. He feels he is no longer a part of it; possibly feels he isn't doing his share or will punish himself by thinking he is no longer worthy of being a part of the team. If ignored, the player will be lost to the team and maybe himself, so he can't be allowed to dis-associate himself from the group of which he has so strongly felt a part. Create ways to keep him in the program and a part of the group.

***

Football, and possibly other team sports as well, has a tendency to delay the college or pro athlete from growing up and facing the tests of adult decisions. The athlete functions as a social being primarily within the team in an atmosphere in which he is protected and insulated from many dilemmas. It is a society where there are guidelines and where there are established and well structured codes of conduct. It isn't until this association with the team is terminated that the former athlete must face simple, everyday decisions without the "team society" to guide him.

***

Ethical conduct should be a matter of principle, values, and an outgrowth of a commitment to the higher moral ground. In truth, there are those who function ethically only because they fear the consequences of doing otherwise. The loss of reputation, employment, friends, and possibly loved ones could be the outcome.

***

Political correctness and moral correctness are similar in many aspects; however, moral correctness in general has an enduring universality to it. Political correctness can change by the generation and/or national borders. What is politically correct in one country may not be in another. Chances are general parameters of morality are not guided by time and place.

***

Every coach who is on the sidelines during a game should work with the defensive backs at least twice a week during the back peddling drills. It is a matter of survival. You have to get out of the way of those sideline pile-ups.

***

Being moral and ethical doesn't seem a natural part of human nature. Religions preach it, but it seems we often need laws to enforce moral and ethical concepts.

***

Winners sometime lose and losers sometime win, but over time a pattern will emerge and an association will be made. One thing for sure, winning is hard work. The work may seem more enjoyable when winning, but it is still hard work.

***

Moving from job to job I only had to move myself. . . my poor wife was stuck with the real moving. When I took a job, I had to get there in a matter of hours to start recruiting. My clothes and me, "on the road again" and so sorry I couldn't help with the planning and executing the move. I really wanted to be there. (Oh Yeah)!

***

Young assistant coaches with young families have a really tough time in college coaching, especially the wives and kids. In all truth it must be like being a widow. All the responsibility of running the home and kids falls on her. And when the season is over, it is then days and weeks on the road for the coach. We always tried to consider the coach and his family as best we could. For the coach it is a labor of love. . .for the spouse it may be the acid that crumbles a marriage.

***

In the recent earthquake in Japan, surviving citizens in and out of Kobe, where the quake hit, shared whatever food or goods they had with those suffering. It was citizen to citizen, not relief organizations or charity. As one commentator put it, what Americans regard as charity the Japanese regard as duty.

***

I have been involved with Japanese collegiate football for a quarter century. Teams I coached played Japanese collegiate teams seven times. The last game we played, they won. I thought they would be elated. They weren't. They were polite, subdued and almost humble. When I inquiried as to why they weren't more excited I was told it was in my honor. Why? In their culture, the greatest honor a teacher can be paid is to be surpassed by the student. We were regarded as the teachers.

***

"If you live by the sword, you die by the sword." Or the run, or pass . . . or whatever. That old standard makes about as much sense as the 'all things being equal' thing.

***

Opportunity won't knock; you must stand by the door and mug it as it runs by.

***

America is an ever-changing society. Demographics indicate great changes in who Americans will be and how they will earn a living in the 21st century. As the variety of our peoples emerge it seems we may become a nation of special interest groups where the majority won't rule, rather parochial interests will. This may or may not be for the best, but it does have the potential to divide the nation, straining and maybe ripping the seams of the patchwork of our nation. Everyone wants the benefits of being a U. S. citizen, but many aren't too anxious to be Americans.

***

In the event the change in attitudes divide rather than unite, then once again team sports will help to bridge gaps and bring us together as a society.

***

A common question asked is, "Who is the best player you ever coached?" Or the best running back or lineman or linebacker? The best coach? There is no answer to such questions. If each and every player and coach was a carbon copy of each other in talent, outlook, etc., then maybe the best could be determined. A running back who is a power runner is apple, the one who is dangerous in the open is an orange. Both may be the best, but not in the same way.

***

We would sometimes have youngsters taken in the pro draft after the sixth or seventh round. They were wanted by the pro team, but not a potential high salaried pick with high powered agents. In those situations, to avoid a commission to an agent, we managed to have a contract lawyer and financial advisor from our law school to review the youngster's contract. It protected kids from sometimes cleaver loopholes in contracts.

***

In 1976 the Detroit Sports Extra named me their National Coach of the Year. Wow! Didn't know who they were, but I accepted. I found out later they were a gambling service and our team topped Division I in busting the odds. Not too many have ever been the bookie's Coach of the Year.

***

Tom Pratt, who was on the Chiefs' staff when I was there, and we were together again in '97 at the Coast Guard Academy. Tom is a three decade veteran of NFL coaching, and his constant battle cry was a constant, "one play at a time." He said it often, believed it sincerely and had players exercising it. The players truly didn't gloat or fret about the last play, or thought about the next one. They played the game one play at a time.

***

Is retribution the same as vengeance? If yes, then is justice only a noble name for the same? Isn't vengeance in the hands of a higher authority?

***

As upsetting as the mouthing, strutting and general lack of respect players have for each other… more deeply it is an attack on the very institution of sport. If the institution of sport isn't appreciated and respected by the participants, then we will have pillars of clay. Organized sport will go on, but will be reduced to the lowest denominator.

***

The Fourth Down

Developing understanding of one's own culture and taking pride in it is important. Others appreciating it is of value to all. However, if carried too far it can lead to polarization and Balkanization. A common language is a key ingredient for a compatible society. Without it enclaves develop that are often hostile toward others and not infrequently toward their own. The danger is neither diversity nor the pursuit of it. . .the danger is that without sensitivity and balance it can become divisive.

***

If human nature stays true to form, the societal issues of age, race and wealth are now joined by gender hostility. However, it is the never ending circle. As each issue is modified an old one returns. If gender hostility does exist, and if resolved. . .then we can expect age, race and wealth to return within each gender.

***

The roots of an enduring marriage aren't romance and passion; it is a matter of loyalty, stubbornness. . . and two bathrooms.

***

The coach who falls into the architect category usually moves from job to job in the profession. It seems building the program is the challenge, not sustaining it. When the creation is in place, it's time to seek another challenge. Maybe this conduct is a result of self-doubt, always needing to prove oneself again and again, or fear the creation won't be sustained.

***

There are two things just about every coach believes about himself. . .that he can win where others have lost, and that he can handle the players others couldn't. Both result from a coach's confidence and ego. This belief is what leads some coaches to take bad jobs.

***

Molly Ivins is a political columnist and satirist for the Fort Worth (Texas) Star-Telegraph newspaper. She has commented that almost weekly there is some study presented about how dumb Americans are. She rejects this. Rather, she says, we all choose "selective ignorance." We choose those things we aren't interested in and ignore them. Individually we have considerable ignorance. Collectively, society should be in pretty good shape.

***

The sociological aspects of athletics, documented and generally accepted, may well be more important than ever to young people. For many youngsters living in high crime areas, athletic teams may be among the few positive groups available to join.

***

In our mobile society, where families can move from one part of the country to another with ease, the roots of the neighborhood are gone. We have become a nation of transients. Neighborhoods with roots seem to be the domain of the disadvantaged: those without the resources to escape. For teenagers, their roots often manifest themselves in gangs, a sub-culture with rules and regulations and who are above all territorial, owning the neighborhood. Athletics can be a counter to this.

***

What is interesting, we are all aware of the problems of society and education to have discipline and a dress code adhered to. . .something the gangs extract from their members without hesitation. Is there something to learn from gangs?

***

Players not informed of their role on the team or not willing to accept it can cause havoc. It isn't unnatural for one player to become envious and jealous of another. It won't subside. . .quite the opposite, each day of practice it is vitalized and grows. It can tear a team apart. Players must know their place, and the coaches must impress upon the squad that decisions on who plays is theirs, not the players. This can help to lower the boiling point.

***

In putting together a game plan there are certain plays for certain situations. It took me a few years to realize that certain plays are really a matter of certain players. In short yardage we would run a certain play. . .in reality the play selected was the one that put the ball in the hands of the back we knew was reliable at getting yards in tough situations. This is what basketball does. . . at the end of the game, when a basket is needed, basketball works a play to get an individual open.

***

When trying to get to a destination but blocked by a horde of people wanting your autograph, here is a system to get where you are going without being blockaded. When I was on the Kansas City Chiefs staff, we had just won the league championship. While heading for the parking lot after the game, wide receiver Chris Burford was confronted by a large number of people crowding around him. He turned around and slowly walked backwards, signing autographs as he backed out. The people, though facing him, were really behind him and Chris went forward by going backwards. . . unimpeded. It registered with me. . . if I was in such a situation I had a smooth way out.

***

A few years later, while coaching at Utah State, we won a big game against a Big Ten team. This was it! I would be overcome with the multitudes wanting my autograph. As I departed the dressing room I saw clumps of people I turned and began to back toward the parking lot. . . pen in hand. . . what did I accomplish? I backed into a lot of people walking to the same parking lot. The moral of the story. . . this technique works only if somebody wants your autograph.

***

No coach really knows if his team is "ready" or not. Coaches like to think so. . .but the coaches are really hoping the team is ready and look for little signs to encourage them, "Them" being the coaches. It is my belief that something happens in the game that sets the "ready" and momentum mode.

***

True, there are games where teams are more excited and acute than others and it can mean little. In fact, being too acute may hamper performance. One time, while coaching at Wake Forest, we played Virginia. Neither team was very good, and this game was one of the few chances either had for a victory. I thought our team would really be ready. Friday's practice was without concentration. At our evening dinner and pre-game meal the kids were loud, laughing. . . almost as though they had no interest in the game. I was beside myself. . .here was a chance to win and our players were someplace else. Wake Forest 63, Virginia 21.

***

A possible way to determine how good a job a coaching staff is doing is determine how many times they have upset somebody compared to the times they have been upset. Of course, a very good team will have fewer chances at upsets because they are winning much of the time and are favorites.

***

Upsets can be misleading. Odds makers and school names can make favorites; the talent playing isn't given enough evaluation. Based on my theory, in twenty-seven years as a college head coach we engineered twenty-nine upsets and we were upset eleven times. However, in a number of those games it was a media upset. . .not talent. We were loaded. Two years in a row, when Utah State played West Texas, long time pros MacArthur Lane and Altie Taylor were the running backs for Utah State and Duane Thomas and Mercury Morris for the Texans. When we beat a Wisconsin or a Kentucky it was considered an upset. It wasn't. We should have won. In true upsets over the career, I think we did the upsetting fourteen times and were on the receiving end four times.

***

We never had a budget that permitted us to send a coach to see a recruit wherever he might live. We assigned coaches to territories and that coach recruited youngsters regardless of position in that geographic area. However, regardless who was recruiting whom, the position coach had to approve the offering of a scholarship. The position coach would review the tapes and determine if he wanted a youngster or not. By doing this, a position coach could never have a disclaimer about a youngster who was a disappointment, blaming the recruiting coach for the error.

***

Consider in obvious quarterback sneak situations switching the offensive tackles to the guard positions. It may provide bigger linemen used for straight ahead blocking.

***

Statistically, going for the blocked punt is better than the return for field position. If committed to this precept and a time comes where a punt return is wanted but a planned return has generally been ignored, the down linemen can remain in the game but the remainder can be the kick-off return team. They have experience in open field returns. With the down linemen holding up the coverage team, there is open field.

***

A major assignment, especially in the pre-season practices, is for the offense and defense to coordinate what they are going to install. In doing this, if the offense and the defense are going to work against each other, one side of the ball shouldn't have an advantage. If the offense is going to work on the double-team block, the defense should have worked on playing against it. . . and not go into a drill and get wiped out. Or in a pass scrimmage the defense is stunting and the offense hasn't prepared for it. If not, there will be bad feelings, excessive exposure to injury and possibly breaking the confidence of players.

***

When working on drop back pass blocking in the early season we wouldn't allow the offensive line to go against the defensive line until the offensive line coach said it was time. Often the defensive line coaches would get impatient, as they were ready to pass rush the first day. Drop back pass protection is among the most difficult techniques to teach and execute. If the offensive linemen are overwhelmed before they are prepared, they may never recover. It's dangerous to throw non-swimmers in the deep end of the pool. If they don't drown, they may never go near the water again.

***

Common language among the staff is a must. The defense must adopt the offensive terminology and vice-versa. If not, much time is lost in meetings and practices while one coach explains to another what means what. On occasion, lack of common terminology can lead to a critical breakdown during the game because one coach can't get a message to another quickly.

***

The flip-flop of the offensive line and the reasons would be a book in itself; however, I am a believer. In a simplistic way. . .it meant better organized practices; more repetitions of fewer assignments, need for fewer talented players and a better opportunity to create mis-matches in the running game.

***

At times it seems there are zealots who use God as a front man for hate.

***

It seems as though all ex-linemen who become head coaches, at any level, want to call the offensive plays. It is their chance to play quarterback.

***

Though temptation may intrude, there are a number of reasons not to cheat. However, if ethics, principles and self-respect aren't enough. . . consider this as the most practical reason of all: if a coach is a party to illegal activities involving a player, then that player is in control of the coach and possibly even the program. The kid can blow the whistle on the coach over anything and at anytime he wants. Compound this with the realization the player can do the coach in years after the player has departed school. The player gets all he can and then sinks the coach years later. So, if honor isn't a reason. . .being in charge of your program is!

***

A coach taking over a new situation, especially when it is a losing one, talks of rebuilding and the time it will take to attract and develop the players needed for success. Right off the bat you are telling the returning players they can't win and the coach doesn't want them. The coach is discouraging the only players he has.

***

Sometimes coaches assume this posture to protect themselves from the public expectation. And many times it is true; but to get the most out of the team, the coach should keep this reality internal among the staff and administrators. . .to the players, give them hope and enthusiasm. Have them focus on the effort it will take to adjust to a new program and a new scheme. This can bring extra effort and direction to the players and makes them feel a part of the change, not temporary participants until they can be replaced.

***

Don't neglect to use your own staff to evaluate what the other side of the ball is doing. With offensive and defensive staffs, one can use the other to get reactions to game plans and strategies. Within a few minutes the offense can present their game plan to the defense and vice-versa. In this way they have outside input to what is planned.

***

Fresh thinking may be generated in the off-season by each side of the ball telling the other what offensive and defensive schemes give each the most trouble. On occasion between seasons we have given the defense a week to construct what they think would be the best of offenses and the offense the best of defenses. What is developed is something based on what each has the most trouble dealing with. After that the discussion centers on what we should consider adopting.

***

There are individuals and teams who love to play but are afraid to compete. There is a difference, and those suffering from failing to compete aren't aware of it. There are good teams talent-wise who fail to have the success their talent should provide. Maybe they just play. . . not compete.

***

There are certain games when the mind tells the emotions to get excited. . . the emotions say, "I know!" There are others where the emotions won't listen. Then the discipline of a focused mind must carry the day.

***

During time-outs on the field it is quite possible a team flopping around loses an edge. Consider having the players take a knee in a huddle formation a yard or so apart. Doing this gives them a chance to relax, get air, be easily reached by managers tending them and to communicate with each other.

***

Most coaches do it, but I have seen games where the coaches on the sideline who may be signaling offense or defense to players on the field are attired the same as the other coaches on the sideline. With the commotion on the bench the coach communicating to the field should be attired in a bright color so he may be easily spotted from the field.

***

If the sideline is sending in offensive plays, the coach should move up and down the sideline, within the coaching box, to be as close to the offensive team as possible. The closer the coach is, the shorter the distance the player has to go and the less time is used. The same with the player leaving the field; get off the field as directly as possible thus reducing the chances of too many on the field when the ball is snapped.

***

We want the player going in, to run with some authority and the player leaving to move quickly and not casually jog from the field.

***

For us, regardless of our overall personnel and strategy, be it run or pass, we had to be able to run the basic off-tackle play. It was the play we wanted our offense to take pride in and the defense had to respect it. We had to be able to execute the tight end and tackle double-team block.

***

Flip-flopping the offensive line was good to us. Here is an example. If we did face a player who was eating our double-team up, if we flip-flopped, the double-team was on a different man. Should the defense flip with us, we worked the double-team from both sides the ball far more than the defensive player had played against it. We delivered the double-team a minimum of twenty times a game using this tactic. Those years we were more a running team than a passing one. . .double the number.

***

Be sure to know who the best skilled position players are and get the ball in their hands. The more opportunities they have to handle the ball. . . the more the chance for something good to happen.

***

It took an in-game experience to realize if the wind is blowing and a player needs to hold the ball on the kicking tee for the kick-off. . . it is much easier if it has been practiced prior to the occurrence in a game.

***

Applying the same rationale to the tackle inside the split end, as done with the tight side end and the tackle, a major concern was to keep the defensive player across from the split tackle from closing down hard to the inside. A change-up for the split side tackle from the direct one on one block is to use pass protection action which should attract a pass rush technique from the defensive player, bringing him at a wider angle and slower pursuit angle.

***

Like most teams, when we practiced offense and defense each wore different color jerseys. A nuance of preparation is to have the offense wear the jersey color they will wear on Saturday. Usually that means the offense and defense will switch jerseys each week depending on the coming Saturday's game. This gets the offense familiar with the Saturday colors.

***

Using automatic timers that sets off an alarm after a certain number of seconds is a tremendous aid in assisting quarterbacks to deliver the ball within a specified time period. It also can serve in the developing of defensive backs in staying with a receiver in coverage.

***

Punters and placement kickers have a prescribed program that includes stretching, weights and various kicking drills. With all of this, time still drags for kickers, and in a way they never really integrate into the team. In the first part of daily practice we included them in the secondary drills. Footwork, agility, and open field tackling not only exposed them to what they may need in a game, it made them a part of the team and accepted as more than just kickers.

***

It's half-time and a team has an out of reach lead. That was always scary to me. I feared a loss of concentration and a casual style of play that would lead to injury of our players. Telling the team to stay alert, play hard, and don't let up is a waste. The zest is gone. You know and they know the circumstances to lose aren't there. Create an objective for the team. An objective can be the opportunity to work on something. . .to make them concentrate. Examples of these objectives: perfect take-off on the snap of the ball; proper offensive and defensive footwork; exact timing. Anything to reduce the game to concentration on detail.

***

Polls, bowls and publicity translate to indifference to the game and the principles of fair play. There are coaches who have lost perspective and join this pursuit for attention by running up scores on hapless opponents. The purpose is to win and dominate the game. . not to humiliate youngsters on the other team. To have the kids on the losing team thinking its a joke ruins the game. Players should respect their opponents. . .trying to embarrass your opponent isn't respect. It's contrary to sport. Even boxing can call the dogs off. . .its's called a TKO.

***

Keep in mind when coaching that you are dealing with somebody's child. Regardless of age. . somebody's child.

***

There are times the academics will bar a youngster from competing because grades indicate the possibility that athletics are depriving the kid of study time. They believe taking sports away means that time will be put to studies. This might be acceptable if the academics would demand the athlete go to study hall or be with a tutor during the normal practice time. They don't. So the athlete now has a couple of hours of free time in the afternoon. I wonder if they go to the library? Or the local pub? Maybe watch the "soapies."

***

My time coaching in Utah was great. The town was about eighty-five percent Mormon. The Mormons seem to live their faith every day compared to other religions. I believe one of the reasons is that their clergy work in the community. The local merchant during the week will be the reverend on Sunday. It seems to lead to a daily practice of religion.

***

How we perceive others very often is not the way they perceive themselves. It isn't uncommon that we may afford them more self-worth than they afford themselves.

***

The most insignificant of things can have the most dramatic of impacts. We had a youngster on our team one time who came from the ghettos of Denver. He was asked by the press one time how he liked being at our school and he replied that he loved it. When asked why, he said, "it is the first time I have ever been called by my first name."

***

As a coaching staff we had a policy of addressing our players by their first names. Our belief was that by doing so we personalized our relationship a little. It let the person, who he is, be a part of the player, what he is.

***

We tried to impress upon our players how unique they were. As best as we could figure, each was an original that had never existed before and would never exist again. A one and only. . .it didn't make sense that they would fight somebody who owed them $10.00 and turn around and cheat themselves with destructive behavior without giving it a second thought.

***

The "big" game, homecoming or the big rival, often leads teams to add special plays and maybe leave what they are doing in the effort to win. Through the years we have been fairly successful in those situations. Focus and execution were primary to us. As a result we reduced our offense and defense for those special games. Our concentration was geared toward execution; confidence in what we do and increased repetitions to do it. Simply, it was a week of "back to basics."

***

As one pursues his career it seems resumés are written; near the end remembrances are written. In order to avoid a complete end to the career. . .don't write the last page.

***

When the pre-game prayer was permitted we never asked for victory. Our plea was to have an effort we could be proud of and to have no serious injuries to either team. God would only be able to bring victory to half those playing and it seemed to usually be the team with the better players.

***

I am not sure God answers prayers by divine intervention. It may be that prayers are answered by providing focus and individual effort to the individual praying to achieve what is being prayed for . . .thus. . ."God helps those who help themselves."

***

The autocratic coach has the advantage of immediate, decisive decisions to be carried out. He may know much about every area of football and not be challenged by staff. . .they just carry out the directions. The delegator may have staff that knows more about an area than the head coach, and the head coach's thinking may be challenged by the staff. The delegated staff may well make better decisions because there is more exchange of knowledge. The autocrat will have less indecisiveness.

***

Coaching has prevented some of the real world from catching up with me, so I have never fully grown up. Thank you, coaching.

***

I remember when applying for a job meant the application was supposed to be sent to a personnel office. Now, I often see that one should forward the application to an office of human resources. Since E-mail makes one-on-one conversation obsolete, job applications are no longer from people, rather resources.

***

There are few coaches I have ever encountered who were satisfied with the number or quality of their offensive linemen. . .they are hard to come by. It is also unusual to go through the season with enough quality running backs. They do get knocked around and the front liners play banged up most of the year.

***

A coaching friend of mine, in Division I, seldom if ever recruited wide receivers or defensive backs. He brought in more quarterbacks and running backs and from there switched to the other positions.

***

Division III college athletics is all over the road in athletic emphasis regardless of their non-scholarship program. Division I and II give scholarships and go out and recruit players. In Division III one school may give no preference to an athlete for admission while another goes out of its way to admit athletes. In theory they are pure. . . in application it is hypocritical.

***

Not too long ago a non-sportswriter on the west coast started his Bottom 10 football teams each week. It got a lot of play and was syndicated. I never thought much about it, other than it being stupid. Then I coached a team that made the list. Wow! It was the most destructive thing I have seen happen to a team. The players were embarrassed and humiliated. They became a joke among their classmates. And there were more than a few alumni on the phones at once, demanding the coach be fired that day. The public humiliation was too much.

***

I took out a $1,000,000 personal liability policy. I vowed if I met the guy I would be arrested for assault.

***

Don't neglect to use the swimming pool for conditioning. Wind sprints can be simulated using the shallow end of the pool. It is easier on the joints and muscles while promoting a strong cardiovascular workout.

***

When I was with the Chiefs, Mike Garrett was a rookie, in practice, every time he carried the ball, wherever it was on the field he carried across the goal line. It was something that impressed me to the point that when I became a head coach, our ball carriers had to do the same thing. When plays were being run for timing and execution we placed the ball on the thirty yard line or less and the ball carrier finished the play off by crossing into the end zone.

***

We seldom scrimmaged during the season, so when the offense went against the defense, we pressured the defense to get to the ball carrier. When they reached him, we wanted them to grab at the ball. This assisted the backs and receivers in securing the ball at all times without thinking about it.

***

Don't laugh.. . .it works! At a set point in the quarterback's count, after the offensive linemen have assumed their stance, have them take a deep breath and hold it until the snap count. The exhaling on the snap count gives more explosion off the ball. The problem is that the coach really doesn't know if the linemen are doing it. It requires constant reminding until it's a habit.

***

Defensive linemen and backers begin to lose their conditioning just before mid-season. Mostly both groups run a few steps and hold up in practice during team time. About mid-season or a little earlier they need extra conditioning.

***

All kick returners should have shoulder pads and helmets on, even in drills, when catching kicks. If not there is a chance the returners will have balls bounce off the pads, or they don't get their heads up properly unless the gear is worn anytime they are receiving.

***

There are times in practice we wanted players to know we would trade intensity and concentration for time. If the players demonstrated these two qualities over a sustained period of time we would shorten the length of practice. This was offered at those times the coaching staff wanted pressure performance in place of learning and teaching.

***

Maybe the coach never knows for sure if his team is ready to play or not. . .the coach had better be! Whatever the game, if he isn't in the game. . .for sure the players won't be.

***

Consider not sprinting more than forty yards in conditioning. Beyond that the chance of pulling a muscle increases, especially for the linemen and backers. We evolved to the thinking that the forty yard sprint was more of a mental test than conditioning.

Most of our sprinting was twenty and thirty yards. We strived for explosiveness.

***

A ten yard sprint is the best measure of explosiveness and quickness. Linemen can keep up with backs at this distance. It is best at such a short sprint to have an electric timer.

***

It took me a while to figure out why our receivers and running backs seemed to have tired legs about a third of the way into the season. With all the running they do during practice, the sprinting afterward did them in. As a result, post-practice was used for blocking drills, etc., for these positions while the others conditioned.

***

Our players lifted weights twice a week during the season. From about mid-season on, the backs and receivers would go to the weight room when we began post-practice conditioning. Getting a head start on the weights cleared some of the congestion in the facility, as well as removing from sight those players not involved in conditioning.

***

Pope Pius XI was quoted as saying, "spirit must dominate technique." It is true of most things and especially true in athletics. If you can do something but won't, then it does little good that you can. The spirit is missing. A good example would be the Viet Nam war. A third world country, having prevailed over the French after a twenty year war took on the military giant of the world and endured. Spirit dominated technique.

***

On occasion, as a substitute for a quick-kick, line up in a formation with three wide receivers to one side. The ball is thrown as far downfield as the receivers can get. One goes for the reception, the other two act as coverage players. You might get a reception; you may get an interference call, or interception is as good as the kick. An incompleted pass just takes you to the next down.

***

<u>Among the worst feelings to have is not to speak up when one should have. . .especially on behalf of another.</u>

***

In practice it is beneficial to always go on the third and fourth count and in the game go on the first or second. In this way, when you change up for a longer count there will be less chance of jumping off-sides as often happens when the longer count is used in a game but the players aren't grooved to it.

***

For about four years we were a veer offense, and that meant running the option. My mind told me how effective the option could be, but in my heart of hearts I never was comfortable with tossing the ball around. It wouldn't be effective unless the pitch man could fly and outrun the defense. And too often the running back was compromised by waiting for the quarterback's decision to keep or pitch.

***

My reservation plus uncertainty for the running back prompted us to exercise more control. The option appeared to be an option but it wasn't. The quarterback, in the huddle, would designate the play as a pitch or keep. . .and that is what was run. As execution and repetitions progressed, the QB could call the pitch and keep the ball, but never calling the keep and then pitching. As a result we seldom fumbled; the running back might be disappointed by not getting the ball on the pitch call. . .but was never surprised with the pitch.

***

In the pre-season, when we had two and sometimes three practices a day we alternated practices, one being all run offense and defense and the other all passing. We believed this accelerated our learning and teaching. We could spend more time on fewer things. This seemed to greatly reduce the smorgasbord of trying to absorb and execute both the running and passing game almost simultaneously. It permitted coaches and players a better focus.

***

The third practice was devoted to the kicking game and concentrated time on the screen and draw. During the pre-season we had a third practice four days a week.

***

There are many resources at a college that can be very helpful to the athletes and the football program. The size of the school may influence the services available. We had new team members meet one night a week for an hour with various resources represented. Each week was a different topic.

***

The Dean of Academics would go over requirements needed to stay in school and graduate, the Dean of Students on the parameters of campus conduct. The campus police would explain their role and procedures; then the city police would do the same. We included the career center, academic support services, health services, residence hall director, financial aids, food services, and special presentations of athletics interest. All of this better integrated the players to the total institution and as a result better citizens with meaningful information.

***

Two schools, with the support of the curriculum committee, granted one hour of academic credit for the weekly course. Where offered, we mandated the players to take a course in the use of the library and study techniques, and sometime during the first year the counseling center administered aptitude and interest tests to the players. All of this impressed upon the youngsters that there was a focus beyond just football and we expected them to take it seriously.

***

College presidents can be a direct influence in the recruiting process, and most will help. When the prospect was on his campus visit we would make sure he met the president. It took less than thirty seconds, just a hello and hope the prospect would attend. This meeting, through the years, was among the most commonly mentioned thing by the athletes. Not that it was the key to their decision, but they were impressed and thought it was special.

***

As do most schools, we tested our players on the pending game. At home we distributed the tests after the Friday meeting and wanted it turned in at the Saturday pre-game meal. On the road the test was given while traveling and turned in upon arriving at the destination. In both cases the graded tests were returned to the players as they entered the dressing room upon arriving at the stadium. This gave them a chance to review any errors when they were most focused.

***

Players were encouraged not to fear an error. We wanted them to regard it as in the best interest of all to correct errors. An error didn't bring ridicule or punishment. Good teaching took place. . .there was another test in a little more than an hour. . .starting with the kick-off.

***

The first fifteen minutes of the Sunday meeting we asked the players to fill out a brief report about the game. We asked them to relate the techniques and blocks that worked best for them against the opponent, what they had the most trouble with, and what their opponents did well and poorly against them. We also asked what went well and what went poorly from a team concept. This would be important for next year's planning as well as motivating improvement with the present players.

***

In the off-season a scout report was prepared for each of the coming season's opponents. Then, when the season started, we had a preliminary plan in place and in the season this gave a starting point, making changes and adjustments from what we had already prepared. We didn't start from ground zero.

***

If the numbers in the program allow for designated scout teams an avenue for better performance in preparation is to have the scout teams attend the other side of the ball when the scouting report is presented. The offensive scout team goes with the defense and vice versa. Being included in the meeting gives the scouts a better picture of what is expected; it improves their concentration and saves prep time on the field.

***

After pre-season and the in-season routine was in place there were fundamental drills we wanted done at least twice a week. Sled routines, footwork drills. . .those techniques and skills we tend to let slide once the time pressures and preparation for games becomes paramount. Fundamentals that often become rote for the players.

***

We conducted these drills during team time. While one group was running the offense or defense versus the scout teams, the second group would divide into their position segments and execute the basics under the direction of a senior player. Be assured the senior knows the techniques required as well as the coach. . .and usually will get more effort than the coach. This segment lasted for about fifteen minutes. When the segment ended the teams switched.

***

After each team has completed this segment, team time continued and both teams devoted the remainder of the session to running the offense and defense. This also met our objective to not have any players standing around.

***

On occasion, after practice when it was time for sprints, all the coaches would leave the field and we would turn supervision of the sprints over to the captains. The players were more demanding of themselves and of each other than when the coaches were in charge. It seems a little coasting with the coaches was part of the game. . .but not among their peers.

***

Video taping has changed the way a game is reviewed and evaluated. Games are available on tape minutes after it is over; practices can be reviewed as quickly as the team and staff get off the field. This makes for better coaching and planning, but I am not sure it doesn't further reduce the human element of the game, thus becoming less a game. Technology reduces the face of man. . .and in some ways the need. As stated before. . .the personnel office has been replaced by an office of "human resources." It has an ominous sound to it.

***

I worked for a coach at one time who was so organized and thorough, combined with an unending work ethic, that I couldn't help but learn a lot of football. The down side of this was I never went on the practice field with any energy. The day's work in preparing for practice eroded the enthusiasm for it. Practice seldom ended when it was supposed to, and the staff meetings after dinner further drained the coaches. For players and coaches it was an endurance contest.

***

There were two lessons I took from this. First, let the players know when practice will start and when it will end. . .and end on schedule. Secondly, arrange the staff schedule so the staff isn't trapped in an office fourteen hours a day. Monday night was a total staff meeting; Tuesday night the offensive and defensive staffs met to adjust the game plan after the Tuesday practice. That was the evening meeting schedule for the week.

***

Our first team on offense was made up of eighteen players, and the defense seventeen. Offense was two centers, six guards and tackles, two tight ends, three wide receivers, two quarterbacks and three running backs. The other side of the ball, being a basic fifty-two team, we had three ends three tackles two nose guards three backers and corners and three safeties.

***

The third person would alternate. The third back would alternate at both running back positions; the third wide receiver or third corner would play both sides. All three players would play both positions, but the primary alternate was the third player of the unit. The second team was comprised of the usual eleven players.

***

This approach seemed a bit cumbersome in the initial stages. However, after working with it for a few days it falls into place; it allows our first line players to get sufficient preparation with a by-product of increased morale as more players are first team. In essence, including both offense and defense there are about thirty-five players getting concentrated attention.

***

During the season we didn't scrimmage during team time. Both offense and defense would go all out for two steps. This gave aggressive initial contact with control and avoided pile-ups.

This two step drill requires discipline and the coaching staff must exercise control from the very beginning. The players have to understand and cooperate with it, especially the defense, as they will be frustrated. The coaches must control the two-step from play one of day one.

***

Every coach knows repetitions are vital to preparation. A way to increase repetitions is to run plays in practice without a huddle. Line up and call the play. Instead of being useless because the defense knew the play, it proved to be better because there was concentration at the point of attack. It is a time when audibles can be worked in to take advantage of a defense cheating too much because they know the play. By not using a huddle almost a third more plays can be run in the same time frame.

***

Self scouting is very important. Not by the coaching staff, but by somebody from the outside, a former coach or a friend coaching at another school. The friend at another school may not have the time; he has his own team to worry about. But have an outsider scout your team. The coach will be surprised at what he doesn't know about his team.

***

There is much to admire in the professional athlete. In spite of what seems to be a selfish, spoiled lot, as athletes they have skill, concentration, take pride in performance, a purity of competition, and they stay until the conclusion of the contest. We are addressing the professional as an athlete, not as a person.

***

Often when the offense takes the ball and drives down the field and is dominating the defense, a euphoria takes over and the team will not be denied. Near the goal line the play calling changes, and too often the offense looks to a change-up. They leave what they had been doing that got them down the field. The defense hadn't taken anything away; the offense gets cute, wastes a play or two, and now it is the defense that dictates the play. More than just leaving the offense that was successful, the most destructive aspect is the loss of focus and mind-set. It can affect the rest of the game.

***

Players were expected to work on football the minute they stepped on the practice field. It would be "on their own," but it would be football. No sitting around or playing around.

***

This is good in theory, but there are players who aren't anxious to get on the field early; taping was done by class, with the freshman first and seniors last. Players, after being taped, didn't want to sit around in the dressing room until practice started and didn't want to go on the field before it started.

***

We designated an area adjacent to the practice field that was the players' space. They could sit there, take a nap, or whatever. It was their safe area. Once on the field football was the first order of business. . .but the safe area belonged to the players. Thirty seconds before the start of practice we blew the whistle to let the safe area folks know it was time to get on the field.

***

Playing on a soaked field is tough on the shoes, then the feet. This can be easily solved by a visit to the local grocery store. "Baggies" over the socks, between shoe and sock will provide dry feet, and on cold days. . .warmth.

***

As a coach, beware if your superiors are fans. Fans are a fickle bunch, and if your boss is counted among them, then you could be dismissed on a whim.

***

As important as taking the ball over on the opponent's half of the field is to victory, so is defeat if they take it over on your half the field. One of the most common ways this can happen is somewhat delayed. Interceptions, fumbles and kick returns are obvious and immediate. Not fielding punts is one of the biggest contributors. Usually it comes four downs later. The average distance added to an unfielded punt is nineteen yards.

***

When the team travels it always concerned me that we were leaving some players at home. On the one hand it is nice for them to have some time off from football while the travelers are away. . .on the other it bothered me that they might feel they really aren't a part of the team. If the squad is big enough and the scout teams are pretty much a unit they can have a Saturday morning practice devoted to preparation for the next opponent. As well as more utilization of time. . . it tends to keep the players on campus and not taking hurried trips home. When playing at home this routine can be done on Friday while the first-liners are going through their Friday routine. I regard it as keeping the team whole so that no one feels excluded.

***

We seldom allowed our first offense to go against the first defense. In part, we didn't want half our team to be defeated. Mostly we wanted to avoid pile-ups and injuries associated with them. The only exceptions were in the pre-season. We had one versus one in goal line situations and in PAT protection.

***

In the passing game, when it involved individual drills such as pass blocking and rushing as well as receivers versus defensive backs, all one on one situations, then we had our best versus our best.

***

A lot of coaches spend time teaching defensive players how to strip the ball from the ball carrier. It sure looks great, opportunistic and can turn a game around. As a coach I wasn't that daring. . . my fear was the player would go for the ball instead of the tackle. . .and miss them both. I have seen that happen more than the ball stripped.

***

It is always surprising how teams that have worked hard on the wrong things can win. . .because they have worked hard on them. They do the wrong things well.

***

A very successful coaching friend of mine said that he never won a game during the season. He won with the off-season program. It is in this program that he developed strength, agility and a work ethic.

***

When I was a grammar school kid there were no organized youth programs like Pop Warner or Little League. In Chicago, where I was born and raised there was a well organized Catholic Youth Organization, (CYO), and they were pretty big in basketball and boxing. In grammar school we had a fifth and sixth grade football team and a seventh and eighth grade team. (In sixth grade I played on the seventh and eighth grade team. My football future looked bright. . .little did I know that was the highlight of my playing career). We practiced and played on a gravel playgound.

***

Football was the game we played. Our neighborhood was a block from a city stadium shared by many high school teams. As far back as I can remember that's where I was every weekend in the fall until I began playing organized football. On a Friday, Saturday and Sunday I saw twelve games. I wasn't home much, but my mother did know where I was. . .not a common occurrence in South Chicago.

***

The College All-Star game in Chicago used to be a big deal. It pitted the NFL Champions against the nation's top graduating college football players. I remember riding the street cars for two hours each way to watch them practice at Northwestern University's Dyche Stadium. Did that about six days a week for three weeks. Sometimes a player would let me carry his gear into the stadium. Those were years before I was in high school.

***

Another vivid memory. . .in 1941 my father was home on leave from the Army. We were listening to the Bears playing the Packers. Dad told me if the Bears won, he would take me to the big inner-city game the next Sunday between the Bears and the Chicago Cardinals. Just a little way into the game it was interrupted with a special news announcement. The next day my father was gone and I didn't get to that game the next Sunday on December 14th.

***

High school coaching is truly most satisfying. The players are at an age where they are really willing and can be developed as players and people. The youngsters will do many of the right things as citizens just to remain on the team. It is a complete trust in the coach, a trust that can not be betrayed. The coach can't under estimate his impact on adolescence.

***

I was twenty-two years old when I received my first high school head coaching job. It was a new Catholic school on the south side of Chicago. It started with just freshmen; a class of 325 and 310 turned out for football. One coach, no equipment and all those kids.

***

Moms made practice pants out of over-alls, with sewn in knee pads and thigh pads. We managed to put a parent and booster group together and a week before the first game we had equipment and uniforms.

***

Our schedule that year was junior varsity teams from the area high schools and we went 3-4. The next year, playing with freshmen and sophomores we played small, private schools, but we played their varsity and went 10-2.

***

I taught history, business and science and the pay wasn't so hot. Some help came from the good priests I worked for, they fed me lunch each day and dinner two nights a week.

***

I had to enhance my income, so in the first year, I clerked at a local drug store from 6:00 p.m. to 11:00 p.m. What I remember most was one night catching a youngster stealing a quart of ice cream. I approached him and he threw the carton at me; it just missed hitting me in the head. I just missed getting what amounted to a brick in the face.

***

The second year, after football season, I drove a cab. Great experience. I would get into the cab on Friday afternoon and didn't get out until Sunday night. Pretty good money when added up; the money wasn't so hot for the hours put in.

***

All kinds of people, problems and attitudes. It wasn't uncommon for one to get into the taxi and ask for the phone number of a "lady of the night." It usually meant an extra ten dollars.

***

I didn't know any and refused to find out. I wasn't that pure of heart. I'd just make up a number and give it to the fare. Sure hope the number wasn't in service.

***

I needed the extra money to get to California to see my one true love. We had met in high school. She had gone west to pursue her acting career. We went together for ten years before we were married.

***

Well, that's not quite true. I went with her for ten years; she didn't date only me for that decade. Obviously she lacked my dedication.

***

Barbara passed away six weeks after our fortieth wedding anniversary. I was faithful to her the whole time. To our friends I was regarded as one who took his wedding vows seriously. When Barbara was asked if she believed I was monogamous she said she did. Why? "Because he is too lazy not to be." (Maybe too afraid).

***

In the locker room we always posted a large "For Sale" sign. In a short period of time the question of its meaning would come up. We would tell our players that just about everybody had a price. What was theirs? What was worth them losing their reputation and being dropped from the team? Simply put the intent was to make them aware of reactions to actions. If they did have a price, make it a high one. Don't lose a reputation for lifting a pen or package of ham a from the local convenience store. . .if the individual was going to sell out, then rob a bank. In either case the reputation is shot and no more team. . .but be big time. . .don't lose what you have for ninety-nine cents.

***

I acquired coaching wisdom at a very early point in my coaching career, and I am more than willing to share it. Wisdom came to me in the form of big tackles and fast backs.

***

Hank Stram is a very interesting individual. When I was on his staff in 1966 my impression of Hank was that of a man with high intelligence, high ego and high fashion. As a coach he was an imaginative man. As a boss he was good. He didn't burden his staff with time consuming-and redundant meetings. The offensive and defensive coaches spent hours in preparation, but energies were focused on getting the job done. This staff wasn't diverted from its mission. He enjoyed his job! Hank spent most of his time putting the offensive game plan together and coaching the quarterbacks.

***

The Dallas Cowboys got a lot of credit for shifting into multiple formations during the 1970's. In 1966 when I was on Hank Stram's Kansas City Chiefs staff he was already working on shifting into multiple sets. The Chiefs didn't use it that year, but he had spent enough time on it to exploit in later seasons.

***

The Chief's approach was to put the tight end in the backfield in front of the fullback and halfback. On signal the tight end lined up on the left or right side; the backs moved to their sets and the wide receivers moved up or back. The whole idea was to reduce the defense's recognition and reaction time which would lead to a breakdown in defensive assignments.

***

When coaching small college football I had run a few plays from the original I formation. All four backs line up in a straight line behind the center. It was originated by then Florida State coach Tommy Nugent and became a featured formation when the Seminole's quarterback was Lee Corso.

***

In 1967 I became the Utah State coach; in the back of my mind was Hank Stram's multiple sets scheme and shifting into it from the stacked I. Near the end of the season we played arch-rival Utah University. We both had outstanding teams. The week before the game we spent ten minutes a day on shifting into formations. Our regular plays, but shifting into the formations. When we ran from the stack-I we ran basic inside plays. Our coaching of the tight end was very complicated. If we ran a play right when he was in the I, he took off left and got out of the way.

***

The plan was to begin our shifting the first series we had the ball in the second quarter. We wanted them to be distracted on the sideline and during the half from the basic game. We won the game. Not from the shift, but a brilliant sixteen yard run by Altie Taylor with less than a minute remaining in the game. How did the shift go?

***

We ran the stack-I for two series in the second quarter; our offensive people came out and said the Ute defense was so mixed up they were running back and forth and our kids didn't know who to block. So, in one stroke of coaching genius I managed to neutralize an opposing defense and our own offense.

***

It appears man tries to establish what creed is God's. God hasn't said what His religion is.

***

When the student-athlete gets in trouble, it is the athletics quotient and the coach who get the heat. The Dean of Students should be just as responsible as the coach for the other half of the proposition. The Dean is as much a failure as the coach if a student goes astray.

***

Something I feel good about is my repayment of debt I always felt I owed. Too many people to mention gave me an opportunity and supported me in my coaching pursuits; it was my plan that if I ever had the opportunity to help others I would. As a head coach I believed it was my duty to support staff members in reaching their goals and advancing in the profession. Fifteen assistants became college head coaches; seven became coaches in the NFL; sixteen coaches who lost their jobs and were unemployed were hired, and over forty young coaches were given the chance to break into college coaching.

***

The great advances in technology were supposed to liberate us from the mundane. My observation and experience has me believing it hasn't liberated, rather harassed and captured us. Now we have the immediate transfer of more and more information demanding immediate response. Add to this the constant intrusion upon work to find out why your desk computer is demanding you respond to its undisciplined calls. Now, with lap computers, or power books as they are called, the opportunity to overwhelm is magnified.

***

As a head coach I seldom socialized with our coaching staff. I am sure I frustrated and angered them on numerous occasions; if I was absent from their get-togethers, then they were free to make jokes about me, laugh at me, gripe about me and cuss about me. They could get it out of their systems without inhibitions. I, too, had a release valve. I always had an older, seasoned coach on the staff who acted as my confidant. A coach who gave me the opportunity to vent much the same as the staff, and when finished he kept it all to himself and paid little attention to what I said. The result was that my frustration point was lowered and all of us went forward on an even keel.

***

A coaching colleague of mine once said that one should change jobs every three years. His contention was that after three years your employer begins to list your weaknesses, not your strengths. Over a span of forty-some years I have had sixteen jobs in coaching. I was either very attractive as an employee. . .or couldn't hold a job.

***

There has been one additional job. After active duty with the Marine Corps, it was too late to get a coaching job. I took a job with a finance company. After two weeks of training I was assigned to retrieve a car because of missing payments. As I tried to talk the driver into giving me the keys he pulled a gun on me. I stood there, facing a gun, demanding the keys. I got 'em! I departed, thought about the situation and realized what had happened. It wasn't even my car, and my salary wasn't very much. I quit that day.

***

In relating the coherent as well as the incoherent of this book I have tried to identify the highs and lows of the journey. Wins, great players, celebrity, Super Bowl, Division I coach, getting fired. . .all had impact, but to ask myself what contribution did I make to the sport? To the kids on our teams? Anything to society? I would like to believe there was a contribution, beyond football, to our players and maybe indirectly that contributed to the society. Maybe not. Maybe the opposite for some.

***

Intercollegiate and professional athletics have been among the first to breakdown social barriers. In the 1920's it was athletics that broke barriers for the children of Polish, Italian and Irish immigrants. A few decades later it was the black athletes being integrated into the all white teams.

***

It would be nice to say it was done in the name of social justice. . but alas. . . it was done in the name of seeking victories.

***

Kansas City, Missouri is a surprisingly nice city to live in. But back in the mid- 60's it had multiple personalities. It identified itself as a mid-west city, a western city and a southern city. Mike Garrett, who was the star running back for the Kansas City Chiefs' first Super Bowl team and a year beyond the Heisman Trophy came back for his second season and was looking for a place to live.

***

Approaching one place to rent the landlord recognized Mike and heaped accolades upon his football prowess. When Mike said that he wanted to view the apartment he was told they didn't rent to blacks. As a very hurt Mike departed, the landlord wished him good luck on the coming season. He was accepted as an athlete but not as a person. Shame!

***

In 1968 I hired a black assistant at Utah State. I acted from awareness, not social pressure. The social issues brought it to my attention; however, I realized there was a need to provide opportunity, and it hadn't been done in the past more because of thoughtlessness than racism. I have been told, though I don't know for sure, that hiring in 1968 was the first or among the very first such hirings among the traditionally white major college programs.

***

As I said before, our present day bent on political correctness can and will change. Moral correctness is rather absolute but it can be eroded for the sake of convenience. It is quite possible morality can be repressed in the name of political correctness.

***

I am pleased when I look back and know I did some right things, if only for selfish reasons. In 1954, I started a black kid as quarterback. The school was about thirty percent black and it had never happened. Some town folks didn't like it. The kid started. It wasn't a social issue. . .the kid was the best quarterback. In that community, at that time, starting that kid was not politically correct. . .it was morally, ethically and athletically correct.

***

In 1959 we recruited the first black football player to Pomona College. Today he is a physician in California. In 1963 we did the same at Pennsylvania's Indiana State College. That young man, the last I heard, was an executive with a major airline. When the youngster went to the local barber shop they refused to cut his hair. I went to the college president and told him. He headed for the barber shop at once. He told the proprietor if the kid's hair wasn't cut, he would see the barber shop was closed. Problem solved. Interestingly, the city of Indiana, Pennsylvania was a stop along the underground railroad that helped the slaves escape the south prior to the Civil War.

***

In 1973 we hired Bill Hayes on our staff at Wake Forest University. He was the first full time black assistant hired in the Atlantic Coast Conference. Within two years all the other schools had followed suit. Bill went on to become a head college coach and presently is among the winningest coaches in the game. I credit Bill with educating me about black life in and out of athletics below the Mason-Dixon line. He has proven the reason I hired him, he's a top-flight coach.

***

Mentioning Wake Forest, permit me to pass along another story. A story of integration. Having taken the job, my wife and I drove to Winston-Salem, North Carolina. We had no place to live and really didn't know our way around at all. We arrived on a Saturday, checked into a motel, and Sunday morning bought a paper. There was a new housing development advertised. A small three bedroom, bath and-a-half home for $1100 down and about $180.00 a month. We decided that since they were new we would buy one and live there for a year or so until we decided where we wanted to settle. We called the realtor and he met us there fairly early in the morning. The first thing he did was explain the open housing laws and that it was an integrated development. We were offended by the explanation. So what? We took the house.

***

Found out we had integrated the neighborhood. The only white folks in the development. It was interesting to be the minority residents. Never have concluded if the neighbors were so nice because we were neighbors or if they really hated us but pretended to be nice. Will never know, we enjoyed it there, but did get a first hand taste of being the out of place guys.

***

I went to Wake Forest with a five year contract. At the end of four years they re-negotiated and gave me a new five year contract. At the end of the first year of the new pact I was fired. From there I went to the Blue-Gray game as executive director. I selected coaches and players for the all-star game.

***

In my second year I selected the local college coach to be on the staff. A black coach at a black college. It would have been a first, but I was shot down by the directors, I did the next best thing I could. . .I selected a player from the college to be on the team. That, too, was a first. The executive director's position and I went our separate ways after that year.

***

Generally, what was done during these years wasn't regarded as politically correct. . .and in some of the situations I didn't go unscathed.

***

A couple of additional efforts I feel good about include recommending a young woman to do the radio color on the football network when I was at Southern Oregon State. She took a theory of football class I was teaching, and did she know her stuff! When the local announcer asked me to recommend somebody to do the color I suggested her. He resisted. . .I insisted. . .he agreed to audition her. He was impressed, selected her and was ready to go. First home game, everything was set. Ten minutes before they were to go on air she told him she had "mike fright" and wouldn't do the color. This was in 1981. Opportunity lost.

***

In 1986 our associate athletic director was a woman who was a tremendous coach. Tennis was her game, but her approach to coaching and understanding of the dynamics was super. I seriously pursued her to coach the running backs. She gave it serious thought but in the end declined. Too bad, she would have done well.

***

One of the most difficult and depressing times for me was in the late 60's and early 70's when sports became a social and political tool in the volatile race relations of the time. Kids were refusing to play for various reasons. For us, in Utah, it seemed especially acute because Brigham Young University was in our area, and BYU was regarded as racist by the black kids. Teams playing BYU were divided. Black kids either refused to play them or had all kinds of discussions about it that distracted the entire team and upset communities.

***

In 1969 our team was not very good. We played Air Force and they dismantled us. They were good, but we played as though we just didn't want to be there. The next week we lost again, and BYU was the next game. I found out that the Wednesday before the Air Force game our black kids were having meetings to decide if they would play against BYU. The meetings went on all the next week. The atmosphere on the field was smothering. The black kids were sullen and distracted. The white kids weren't hostile about what was happening, they just knew it was serious and they didn't know what to say or do . . .so they said nothing. Practices were silent. Nobody knew what to say. One group chose to say nothing and the other group didn't know what to say.

***

Sunday afternoon, before the BYU game, the team captains came to see me. One of the captains was a black youngster who was really torn. As a black man he felt he had to stick with the group; as a captain he knew he had an obligation to the team. He announced to me that he would play, but none of the other kids would. I told him I wouldn't do that to him. That he had to do what he could live with.

***

That evening a group of the black players visited and told me they were going to play, that Utah State and the coaching staff had treated them well and they knew their educations were on the line. They reasoned they were punishing Utah State if they didn't play. They were right; BYU had about seven teams on their schedule go through this ordeal. While other teams were coming apart, BYU was under siege and a cohesive unit; it was them against the world. We played and we lost. It was a difficult time.

***

Two interesting asides: in 1968 we had a great running back named Altie Taylor. He and O.J. Simpson were regarded as the premier senior running backs in the country. A week before the BYU game some organization in California called Altie and lobbied him hard not to play against the Cougars. As the story was told to me the calls were many and at times ugly. Finally, Altie told them he agreed with them. He said that he was told he would get a contract in the pros worth about $200,000 a year. He said if he refused to play he would be regarded as a trouble maker by the pros and his market value would go down. If the organization would place that amount of money in the bank, in his name, he wouldn't play. Altie signed with the Lions and had a fine pro career.

***

In 1969, when our team was really disrupted, Steve Kinney, our tight end, who played a number of years with the Chicago Bears, was opposed to boycotting the BYU game. Much later in the year we talked about it. His position was a selfish one. He believed the people on the outside who were agitating the players to not play were exploiting those players. They were asking the players to put up everything while they were putting up nothing. Steve believed his education was the most important thing. His quote still rings in my ears, "I won't go back to San Jose and be on the streets among the unemployed."

***

Nothing can match the tragedy of 1970. Wichita State was on their way to play us at Utah State. They were coming in two chartered planes; one crashed, one arrived. The following sixteen hours were the most crushing and helpless time I have ever known. Parents calling to find out if their child was dead or alive. . . answering that would be as tough as anything could be. . .and that was compounded. The planes were re-fueled in Denver and players from one plane changed with others. . .who was on what plane wasn't known. The players arriving didn't know the other went down until it landed. The players were in shock, some being taken to the hospital. The town of Logan, Utah opened up to them. Every church in town opened its doors in minutes; without any official request dozens and dozens of cars appeared at the motel housing the surviving players. Families took the kids to their homes to comfort them and help them call home at once. Our players sat up all night with theirs. The next morning they were to depart at 5:00 a.m. to Salt Lake City to take a commercial flight home. All of our players were there with sweet rolls and orange juice for them. It was absolute silence but the emotion was screaming. I found out later the college cooks came in at 3:00 a.m. to make the rolls. It is so vivid and fresh to me, as I relate it here, over three decades later, I am crying.

***

The most lasting and memorable high occurred in 1971. In 1970 I was invited to Japan to conduct football clinics for U.S. Service teams and Japanese coaches and visit the Viet Nam wounded in military hospitals. While there I met a Japanese coach by the name of Ken Takeda. Ken received his doctorate from Michigan State and received two Fulbright Scholarships. Ken, one of the top clinical psychologists in Japan, has been president of a Japanese university. . .but his passion is football.

***

While visiting the hospitals I got the phone numbers of the wounded from Utah and promised to call their families upon my return. One youngster, a Navajo, had been a boxer along with four older brothers and he was the most talented. He had lost his arm and he wanted me to tell his family how sorry he was that he would no longer be able to box and bring a life to his family off the reservation.

***

I called the mother of a Hispanic lad who had been shot in the hand. He was fine and would be home in a few weeks. Both of us were shocked because my call was the first notification she had that her boy was wounded, she became unglued. When the conversation concluded, my wife, who was listening, told me something wasn't right and I should call back. For two hours I got a busy signal. Finally I got through. The woman thought I said the wound was to the head. She was trying to call Japan. It was good I called back. To this day I receive a card each Christmas from that mother.

***

The moral of the story. . .no matter what anyone might say, football ain't war.

***

Japan was playing football well before World War II. There are about 300 universities playing football and a well developed industrial league.

***

Coach Takeda said that his dream was to someday have a U.S. college team play against the Japanese teams. This never had been done. It started there. It was agreed if we could get there they would take care of our expenses while there. So it began.

***

To raise air fare I wrote letters to service clubs in the smaller communities our players were from, asking if they would share the air fare costs; the youngster could speak to each group about his experiences. We had forty former Utah State players playing in the NFL and Canada. I asked if they would sponsor a kid. All but one player contributed, some supported two or three players. One of our players sold his truck. He reasoned he could get another truck, but not easily get two weeks in Japan. We raised enough money so that all players who wanted to go could; all the coaches and their wives, and fourteen married players brought their wives.

***

On December 18, 1971 we were in Tokyo's Olympic Stadium to play the first game in Japan by a U.S. college team. Standing there with our National Anthem playing, the goose pimples were really grapefruit pimples. After the game we went to Osaka, saw much of Japan, and on Christmas Eve our hosts held a Christmas party for our group. It included gifts, Christmas carols and candlelight ceremonies. On Christmas we played in Osaka and two days later returned home. It was very special.

***

While in Japan our players spent a few days living in the homes of the youngsters they were going to play against. A great and lasting event. In fact, a few years ago, some of our players who made the trip took their wives and children and went to Japan to visit the players they had competed against and their families. After the recent Osaka-Kobe earthquake I received letters or phone calls from a number of our former players inquiring about the welfare of their Japanese friends. The common theme was that they tried to call and couldn't get through. Those are friendships that have endured for a quarter of a century.

***

In 1985 our Southern Oregon State College football team traveled to Japan to play Kwansei Gakuin University. Among the many activities our hosts arranged was a joint trip by both teams to Hiroshima and the Peace Park. Most of the Japanese players hadn't been there. I had concern as to what reaction there would be between the players of the two teams.

***

We walked the park, tolled the peace bell, saw the mound where the ashes of thousands are gathered. . .then walked through the museum itself. . . with its artifacts and pictures. It is a nearly overwhelming experience.

***

The joint visit by the two teams had a reaction not anticipated. It brought these young adults closer together. They were in unison in their reaction to viewing the history and pictures of the first atomic bombing. They almost became as one. No guilt among the American kids and no resentment from the Japanese players. They reacted in a hopeful way. . .and as one, it seemed they understood the impact far beyond the parameters of a past war.

***

Akira Furukawa is the commissioner of the American Football Association of Japan. For over thirty years he has worked to establish Japanese collegiate football and has been instrumental in the development of the company team league and the growth of high school football. Through his efforts a Japanese football Hall of Fame recently opened in Osaka. Under his guidance the national collegiate championship game has an attendance of over 60,000. In 1970 it was drawing under 10,000.

From our first trip for a college game between an American and Japanese team we had seven young coaches from Japan come to the U.S. and work in our program for a year or two. Four became head coaches in Japan.

***

International Understanding Through Football is the brain child of Ted Suzuki. He is president of the Suzuki International Corporation and regarded as the all-time best quarterback in Japanese college football history.

***

He is truly a citizen of the world; an international businessman and a friend of high government officials all over the world. . .but his passion is football.

***

He has been a behind the scenes force in the international football between Japan and the United States. He truly believes football displays the American spirit and wants the young Japanese exposed to it. He believes it was America, after World War II, that assisted Japan in creating the economic Goliath it is today. He wants the young people of the two nations to know each other and each other's culture so the bonds will remain strong in the future. His motives are noble, his vehicle is football.

***

I remember being with him one time in the Atlanta airport. There was a large number of Vietnamese refugees waiting for a flight to somewhere in the U.S. They were squatting down and huddled up close to each other. I remember his comment, "America has done more than its share as a world citizen."

***

In 1971 when Utah State made that first international collegiate trip we were staying in a Tokyo hotel. The second or third evening there a local resident came to the hotel and asked to take two of our black players out for dinner. I was hesitant but agreed.

***

When the youngsters returned they had loads of gifts and the players said the man must have spent more than a thousand dollars on them. Why?

***

Upon returning the players to the hotel, he told them he was visiting family in Hawaii when Pearl Harbor was attacked. Being a Japanese citizen he was interned and not allowed to return to Japan. He was assigned work in a military dining hall cleaning tables and picking up. He said that the only American servicemen who treated him with any dignity were the blacks. This was his first opportunity to repay that kindness.

***

Recently I was invited back to two schools where I had coached. One where we won few games and the other where we were very successful. In both situations it was over twenty years ago and the players, for the most part, were now middle-aged. The players humbled me in their support and comments. From that experience I have come away believing I have done some good in a way I had aspired to do.

***

So many of those who coach have been influential in a young person's life, often far more than realized. In some cases the coach has become a proxy parent. . .and in many situations assisted parents in directing their child. . .sometimes with, but most times without either party knowing it. The coach hasn't made a smart kid smart nor a doctor a doctor. . .what the coach has done is keep a maturing individual in a positive environment. . .providing direction, supporting standards, exposing the youngster to obligation and responsibility. . .the coach is often the "wind beneath the wings."

***

A career in coaching is a precarious one, even for successful coaches. Victories can't be deposited anyplace to be withdrawn when needed at a later date.

***

In reflecting upon my attitudes as a coach through the years I can chronicle how they changed. As a young head coach the time between games from week to week seemed an eternity. I was as excited as any player on game day. I just wanted to stand in one spot and jump up and down. A win was euphoric.

***

My next phase was going into games confident of what we were doing and confident in our players ability to perform. It was exciting to win, but more matter of fact and expected. My feeling going into the game was enthusiasm but guarded.

***

After a few more years and after decent success, entering the game was a bit more grim. In most of our games we were favored to win; we expected to win and that was a different kind of pressure. Week after week, to meet expectations, while knowing there would be a stumble or two along the way. Victory didn't bring excitement or joy. . . it brought relief that we hadn't stumbled.

***

At Wake Forest wins were hard to come by. My attitude evolved into a hostility. Just about every game we went into I believed we could win. But as a coach I entered with a heavy heart, knowing it was an uphill battle. Losing wasn't an upset . . it was expected by our fans and I think our players . . . and maybe down deep by me, but I think it was suppressed if it was alive. After the game the energy focused on keeping the team together and to keep them battling.

***

The final phase, when we were winning more than we were losing and I was a few years older, I was more clinical in my approach to the game and more matter of fact after it. Winning was satisfying it meant that our preparation and execution had been successful. A loss didn't lead to depression . . . it meant an immediate focus on the next opponent without any delay. Win or lose the juices flowed. They flowed as a part of a process.

***

Career aspirations are individual and pretty well understood by the coach. Achieving these aspirations can be enhanced or aborted by the planning, preparation and effort of the individual. There is a truth to being in the right place at the right time. . .this is a circumstance that usually comes about without warning.

However, when it does take place the coach better be able to recognize it in the total scheme and be able to perform.

***

It is vital for the aspiring coach to know the limitations that may or may not exist in his pursuit. Coaching is a profession that requires mobility. . .moving is common. My career has taken me from Illinois to California to Pennsylvania, New York, Arizona, Missouri, Utah, North Carolina, Alabama, Oregon, Connecticut. . .and where next?

***

If there are limits to freedom of movement the coach must recognize them and live with them. Family may dictate limitations, or a refusal to move from a certain geographic area can limit upward mobility. What price is the aspiring coach willing to pay? For me, it was a wife with a successful career and not having kids. She helped me chase my dream and the price was nearly a decade of me coaching all over the country without her joining me. Our marriage endured but it was sure challenged.

***

For me, an independent spouse and no children provided me with latitude many don't have. Was chasing my dream worth the separation and risk of losing my wife? Now, many years later, I ask if it was worth it. I have to say yes. . .but presently I achieved what I pursued and the marriage survived. I might have a different opinion if either half of the equation had failed.

***

In pursuing a job one can't be intimidated by the competition. Often the final selection is a compromise candidate. One group may be backing a top candidate while another group is supporting another. If either gets the job, then one significant segment of support is alienated and may withdraw. It isn't uncommon for both sides to agree on a third person; in this way neither side got "their" choice and neither side withdraws.

***

Keep in mind, the job description is perfection and man isn't that. If the previous coach was discharged you can bet they will try and replace his weaknesses. If your research goes well, you may know what those weaknesses were.

***

Go to coaching clinics and other professional activities as often as you can. Go out of your way to meet coaches. Over a period of time they come to know who you are even when all you did was say hello.

***

Be aware of your conduct at any gathering. You don't know who is watching or who will be the next coach to get a good job. At times, with peers, I have seen young coaches look like bums; sometimes act like bums. . .maybe have too much to drink in public. When with a circle of friends one might forget others may be viewing and it can come back to haunt the job pursuit. I may be prudish, but I admit I didn't hire coaches who applied for a place on our staff because I have negative recollections of their conduct.

***

The best time of the year for the college jobs is in December and January; then another little burst will take place in late spring and early summer. The spring job openings are fewer in number but the competition is reduced since most coaches are employed and would hesitate to leave a staff at such a late date. High schools open most frequently in winter and early spring.

***

When you are on the hunt and a job opens, do the best you can to research it and know something about it. Is the job open because the coach has moved on? Or has he been let go? If a successful coach moves on there is a good chance an assistant on that staff will have the best shot. The successful program seeks continuity.

***

If the coach was let go, try to find out why. Did he function in such a way that he brought it on himself? Was he in a poor situation? Sometimes, in the eagerness to coach, we take bad jobs. . .and the eager coach discards the realities, relying on his belief he can win where others have lost. In the simplest of terms, if the coach was let go for losing. . .why did he lose?

***

Research resources the program has; location in terms of recruiting; admission standards; is the administration stable? Strength of schedule; coaching turnover in the high profile sports. Do assistants endure or is there high turnover? Some administrators scapegoat the coaches by firing them to keep pressure off themselves. Some head coaches do the same with assistants.

***

An assistant coach should know his role and what is expected of him, not just on the field but off as well. The head coach can expect loyalty. . .the paycheck purchases it. The assistant, by working as best he can for the head coach, in reality is working for himself. He becomes a valued staff member.

***

Does the assistant get responsibility? Are the assistants on the staff known for their particular contribution, or is it a one man show? If the assistant has earned the respect of the head coach will the head coach assist the assistant in his career pursuits? Is the situation and modus operandi one the assistant can function in or not?

***

Before taking the job the assistant should talk with the head coach to be sure they are on the same page. The discussion should reduce as many future surprises as possible. Not everything can be anticipated, but one would be foolish to go in blind.

***

The first time head coach needs to seriously analyze himself honestly. What intrigues him most about coaching? What style of supervision best fits his personality? Above all he must recognize his weaknesses. . .in coaching and in personality.

***

The head coach, when putting his staff together, should make every effort to hire to compensate for his weaknesses. But above all. . .hire good people. Expect loyalty and demand it. The easiest way is to employ loyal folks.

***

Disagreements aren't disloyal. They can help growth. Disagreements can become disloyal depending on the forum in which they are expressed and the reaction of the individuals to them.

***

Some coaches, anxious to climb the coaching ladder, seek out and almost pander to those they regard as being the prestige coaches, while at the same time ignoring those who are in the same boat they are. Big mistake! An ignored peer may be in a position to hire you before vice-versa.

***

When the interview is yours, if at all possible, try to be the first or last candidate interviewed. The selection committee is eager and listens to the first candidate and the same for the last. . .because it is soon over. All those in between often become a blur.

***

In the interview, interview as well as be interviewed. Have questions based on the research. Don't be afraid to ask the tough questions; such as why the last coach departed. Even if you know. . .hear what they say. Not rude inquiries, but pertinent ones and those that let the committee know you have given thought to the post.

***

Coaching at one level and having success isn't the usual way you move up to the next class. It can happen, but more often success at one level makes the winner an attractive candidate at that level. If a coach wants to be a Division I coach, then he must work to get into it. This is where contacts count.

***

If you are going to apply for a job, don't call collect to inquire about applying. I have had it done to me more than once. (Needless to say, that was one less applicant to consider). Protocol says it isn't good form to send a letter of application in your present employer's envelope and their stamp. The letter itself should be on plain paper, but the school stationary may at least attract some attention. If where you are is more valuable than who you are. . .take a chance and use the letterhead.

***

Staff members are elements; putting these elements together creates a chemistry and that chemistry should be positive and is felt by the staff and the players. The end result should be the elements mixed together create a positive whole.

***

The head coach should be sure to talk with his staff-to know them as individuals aside from their coaching. Help them establish and reach their career goals. What is it they want? Football is demanding in time, effort and emotion; the coach and his family must know the head coach realizes the sacrifice all are making. It doesn't eliminate the demands. . .but all know the head coach is sensitive to it.

***

I have known coaches who put in time beyond the need. There were diminishing returns. I believe this was a crutch, so if things didn't go well he could rationalize he couldn't have worked any harder. Don't confuse hours with work.

***

One coaching friend of mine would never leave his office during the season before midnight except Fridays and Saturdays. Whatever he did. . .I don't know. . .his rule was no assistant could leave the office before he did. These were coaches with families (he was divorced), and they would sit in their office three or four hours a night, five nights a week. . .just waiting for midnight so they could go home. Two things happened. . .he had a high turnover in staff and he was fired for losing.

***

Then comes the next phase of coaching. . .getting fired. It is more than a routine of the profession. . .it is assumed to be a part of coaching. A head coach in college will last in his career as a head coach under six years.

***

Two close to home illustrations. . .I was at Wake Forest for five years, one of seven members of the Atlantic Coast Conference at that time. In my five years there were three coaching changes. . .and in year six three more. For nine years I coached in a fourteen team non-scholarship league in Washington and Oregon. At the end of the nine years there were only three coaches still active from the time I began.

***

After being fired there is anger, embarrassment, self-doubt and frustration. . .often a coach fired has done the best coaching he has ever done. . .sometimes the corner has been turned. . .but the rewards a year or so into the future. It isn't just losing a job. . .it is being jilted by a true love.

***

If the fired coach wants to stay in coaching he had better get back in the race. And don't expect great help from your coaching colleagues. . .if the coach wants to coach again, then he had better get it together.

***

Develop a plan to put yourself in a position to pursue a job. Inventory your ambitions, strengths and where you want to pursue a job.

***

Contact your coaching friends to let them know you are looking. Consider returning to school to pursue an advanced degree. Volunteer to coach; attend clinics and conventions.; be seen. . .be available. . .be ready. . .and be relentless. The fired coach will be forgotten in a hurry. . . if he lets it happen.

***

There are so many talented coaches who are prepared, have a plan, paid their dues and never get the break they have given so much to reach. However, the goal must be prepared for. . .because one just doesn't know in advance where and when the right place and time will mesh.

***

There are some in the coaching profession who played at the right school for the right coach who got them started in coaching in the right job. They have gone to the top and claim they never asked for a job in their career; they were always sought for a position. They think they have been touched on the fanny by a magic wand. Maybe they have. There are a few who believe it would be degrading if they initiated contact for a post.

***

I have had a lot of jobs. There is not a single coaching position that I didn't apply for. . .true, I had a lot of help from a lot of people. . .but the application was initiated by me. For every job I have secured I have had multitudes of rejections.

***

Anger and discouragement must be managed. At a point it has to be submerged and the pursuit begun. There is a job out there. . .but it has to be identified and attacked. Nobody but the primary party can do it. In the end, being rejected for a position and not applying have the same result----no job. The difference is a simple one, by not applying the outcome is assured.

***

This is redundant, not unique at points in this book, but I can't help but believe all this attention to diversity, ethnicity and political correctness is generated by an apprehension lurking in the sub-conscious. The human species needs to feel worth. Importance. Value. They need identity. There is something telling us we are losing that identity.

***

Computers talk to people for us. They write us letters. We can shop, bank and communicate through technology. We have less and less interaction one on one. The machines can isolate us from others of our species. Though the machines can do more for us faster than we can do for ourselves, it isn't liberating, it is isolating.

***

As a result maybe there is a survival instinct that drives us to repudiate the total society but seek others of likeness to maintain an identity, which means a value. And to further justify our identity we attack others. We, whoever 'we' is, are victims, and we are being oppressed by some other victims.

***

The "Office of Human Resources" has a demeaning tone. Resources are either renewable or expendable. We're expendable. I am sure there are tax lawyers who are right now putting the formula together that will take into account the productive years plus total salary anticipated over the years, and the next thing we know businesses will be depreciating us each year as an expendable resource. They already do it with pro athletes. In the end corporations can then have a write off on the total value of their contributions in salary and benefits. The individual has enriched the organization without any cost to it.

***

If I listen to the popular theme I should feel guilty about being white, being male and being an oppressor. . .if not in fact, then an oppressor because I am a white male. What I am guilty of is not feeling guilty.

***

One of the key projects we strived for was to have a football player or a friend of a player on every student committee a college had. Over the years we were quite successful with this. The idea wasn't to control anything but to know what was going on, and if there was anything deemed negative to the program, especially based on ignorance or mis-information, we were in a position to defend ourselves.

***

As a staff we tried to have our athletes involved in student government and be aware of the leadership candidates. There were always some who ran on a "cut athletics" ticket. We wanted our players to vote for whom they thought best. . .not just best for athletics. Many colleges elect very radical student leaders because few students vote. The crusaders can win because they rally what few voters there are and the indifferent majority surrender their representation.

***

Most colleges have between three hundred and five hundred intercollegiate participants. That is a pretty significant number to woo. And in most cases, wooed they are.

***

Newsletters were sent to the faculty and staff to keep them informed on what was going on within the program. At times the letters would be returned by a few with caustic remarks. That didn't discourage the effort. The information put forth wasn't a hard sell; we tried to communicate items that weren't controversial or too partisan. The emphasis was on the programs to encourage academic and social responsibilities, those things that avoided debate and would be hard to condemn.

***

Every January the nation's football coaches hold their convention. It is a noisy, active four days. Young coaches seeking opportunities for advancement; middle-aged and older just looking for a job and the elite few who remain in their suites to avoid the pandemonium the lobby incubates. It is an enjoyable few days if you are a coach with a job; if not working, and it is rather a time of job seeking, then it can be a very depressing few days. Very depressing.

***

Observing the scene I created the All-Lobby Team. To make the team the coach must remain in the lobby ten hours a day; circle the lobby hourly; spend fifteen minutes each hour greeting everyone stepping out of the elevator and having himself paged at least four times a day. And, have an accurate list of every hospitality room at the convention.

***

A number of us had a lot of fun with this undertaking for a number of years. Found out later some "really big timers" frowned on the effort. They must have believed they didn't earn their positions, rather were pre-ordained.

***

I was attending the annual football coaches convention at a time the Kansas City Chiefs were looking for a coach. Lamar Hunt and Jack Steadman, the Chiefs owner and general manager came into the hotel lobby when I was there. They were coming in to interview somebody for the job. I knew them from the time I was an assistant with the Chiefs. I greeted them; walked across the lobby with them; got on the elevator with them. . .got off at my floor; went to my room and came back downstairs an hour later. I never denied the rumors.

***

A couple of walls in my office are covered with pictures that represent some special memories and highlights of my coaching career. It's nice. . .but it is also a hollow feeling to realize after a number of years of one's life can be summed up on a wall or two.

***

Each game, in itself, is like a small but complete society. The production of the society is based on the talent and execution the individuals bring to the game. The rules of the game represent the laws of the society and the sinew that provides civility to the society is sportsmanship, another word for respect of self and others.

***

In some games it seems that sportsmanship is eroding and if that is true then sports is giving up one of the pillars for its justification.

***

In most games each play has one side trying to present problems to the other and the answer must be given instantaneously. In the classroom you have a chance to consider the problem; contemplate the answer then present it. Often you have time to change the answer. In sports, Right or wrong. . .Answer now!

***

One may think being an elitist is a birthright and another as an earned right. Both may be insufferable but only one is a fool.

***

I do believe when we pray that something good will happen, we energize ourselves to do our part to see that it does.

***

Though it has been said, "many times, many ways," a fundamental principle of dealing with others is not to challenge their dignity. Their worth as a human being. It may be in order to attack attitude or to attack performance. . .but not dignity. Would you tolerate your dignity being attacked without response? I think I adopted this position when I realized the response might be me. . .knocked on my fanny, sitting in the middle of the field. Result: lost dignity regained by one party and dignity lost by the other.

***

Much of the violence we see in the world against authority, from nations to neighborhoods, may not be a rejection of the authority itself. . .rather significant segments of the population resent how the authority is being exercised and lack the patience and/or knowledge to work through the system.

***

It is exciting to hear fathers extol the skills of their daughters as athletes. Twenty years ago it was only the sons who represented family pride for athletic performance. Not anymore and that is terrific.

***

I can see it now! The big game of the year with State U. and its corporate logo playing U. State with its corporate insignia. They line up for the kick-off, but State U. walks off the field. They stage a wildcat strike against their competition because of unfair labor practices. Or maybe the employees go on strike because their logo had a bad season. Or something like that.

***

Somehow it seems the business of college athletics is more and more about attracting the money to support the program rather than a program the institution can support. Soon, if a school doesn't get a "big bucks" logo they will be squeezed out of the competition. After all, who would pay to see Nike playing Joe's Fresh Produce.

***

Charging into the fray as the Wake Forest football staff, we were going to change the loser into a winner. We needed a quarterback quickly to engineer our air attack. Mike Ellison, one of our young assistants had a friend who was a quarterback on a Division III team in California that had just dropped football. The quarterback wanted to join us. No way a Division III quarterback could play for us. He didn't, we didn't take him. The quarterback did go on to play; many years for the Seattle Seahawks, he went by the name Jim Zorn.

***

Then, a few years later, Jack Kemp, former pro quarterback, U.S. Congressman and later a cabinet member walked into my office telling me of his son and inquiring if we would be interested in him. I told him we had no scholarships open. So, the kid, his son Jeff, played in the Ivy League and had a long and steady career in the NFL.

***

Super Bowl XXXI, a commercial cost $40,000 per second. It seemed the game may have interfered with the advertising sweepstakes and the half-time show sure didn't enhance the event.

***

Recently I attended the annual convention of the American Football coaches Association after missing for a few years. It was amazing, the turnover in such a short period of time. I hardly knew anyone, but what really hurt. . .they didn't know me!

***

It used to be a winning season didn't garner honors for a coach, however, it did keep him employed. Not anymore! Seven wins might get a team to a minor bowl and that isn't good enough. Now the magic number is eight wins and a place in the bowl alliance. In the 1996 season, when Notre Dame lost to Southern Cal it cost Notre Dame $8,000,000 with the loss of alliance participation. What principles are challenged by that kind of money?

***

To prove my consistency, after a junior varsity season, we had a red-shirt quarterback who did well. A really good touch passer. We determined he hadn't a strong enough arm to carry us. After the season I told him I didn't think he would play for us. He had two years of eligibility remaining and if he wanted to transfer now was the time. He decided to stay; in January I was dumped. Two years later he led the team to a bowl game; was the Atlantic Coast Conference Player of the Year and had an NFL tryout.

***

In a way, he is indebted to me. I saved his career. Come to think of it, based upon quarterbacks, maybe I would have fired me, too.

***

One thing I noted through the years, from high school through the pros, the Afro-American players always had time for little kids. Regardless of the color, those players before and after practice, would have time to talk to and play with the little kids and the kids gravitated to those players. Maybe it was the innocence of the little ones or the players having grown up with extended families, this relationship was a common occurrence.

***

It's so confusing! There are laws being passed that if a child transgresses the parents can be held responsible and even jailed. If the parent spanks the child, the child can be removed from the home and the parent put in jail. Wanna go to jail? Then discipline your kid.

***

If a spanking is child abuse, then my mother was a "three strikes and your out" winner before I hit kindergarten; heck, maybe before I was even housebroken.

***

In grammar school and high school, if getting smacked by the teacher was child abuse. . .then, by myself I could have wiped out an order of nuns and a whole slew of Christian Brothers;. . .and of course, you can bet I never deserved to be corrected.

***

I do have an uneasy feeling about the future of football. In Division I the need for revenue has become such a dominating factor that it is difficult to regard it as anything less than a commercial enterprise. This fuels less support for the coach's job; tempts the coach to circumvent the rules and puts more pressure on the athletes to be year-round players. And, don't think there isn't a trickle down effect. Though benefits for the coaches are less and a dollar surplus is non-existent, Division III coaches are bid farewell at nearly the same rate as their Division I counter-parts.

***

So very much time and energy is devoted to recruiting in college that I fear we tend to ignore the kids already in our program. We are working so hard to be attractive to potential replacements for the players we have. . . we don't keep nurturing those who have already cast their lot with us. Don't forget to be thankful for what you have.

***

Keep the faith! After eight years out of coaching and beyond sixty-five of age and hope to coach again. . .it happened. In fact, two job offers on the same day. Now, that was prayers answered. The question: did God help me or did my prayers drive me to help myself? You can't quit if your dream is still alive!

***

There are so many people who do good things for others and we never hear about it from the media. Catastrophe and mayhem is the news pushed. When we are made aware of good things our spirits soar. I have always believed if some daring soul would put on a weekly television show about the good people do for each other, it would shoot to the top in the ratings.

***

If the president of the college or the high school principal wants to give the team a "pep" talk before the game. . .be sure it is a game you will win. Be sure! Such talks by outsiders tend to ignore size, speed and experience. The team loses and its your fault, coach. . . the boss told them to win.

***

One thing I noted from my inspirational "pep" talks to the team. . . they seemed to work best when my players were better than the other guy's.

***

Wake Forest is a fine university and a good Baptist school. Our teams were poor; we prayed a lot. From this my theology reached the conclusion that I didn't know God's religion. . .but it's not Baptist. Heck, I stopped our pre-game prayer. We were making atheists out of those kids.

***

In seeking one thing or another, I have made so many deals with God I couldn't come close to keeping track. It usually goes, "if You will do this----I'll do that." It seems quite often He did and I didn't. Being omnipotent, I am sure God knows when I try and make a deal I am lying. . .even if I don't know it at the time.

***

Junior college athletes can provide a program with quick help, so it is thought. We operated a program that was dependent upon junior college transfers for the bulk of the team. We were careful to recruit those with a decent junior college academic record. In that way we had a player with proven experience and a student with a proven college academic record.

***

Two things we found out with the junior college athlete. He was easier to recruit than the player just out of high school. The JC youngster is more mature, usually has been through the high school recruiting experience and knows the move from a two year to a four year school is pretty much a final move as far as eligibility is concerned. The maturity makes him more aware of realities and he is less confused. He may not be quicker to say yes. . .but he is in saying 'no.'

***

What we did find out that it was best to "red shirt" as many of the junior college transfers as possible. They really had difficulty picking up the offensive or defensive system in one season; however, more than that, the JC player just doesn't feel comfortable in the program that first year.

***

Financially the junior college player even as a 'red shirt' is a pretty good investment. Three years of scholarship cost for two years of play compared to a frosh, who will usually get two years of play for a four year investment.

***

We were playing Duke in Durham. We didn't take the field for the pre-game warm-up. We won the game. Some thought it a brilliant psychological ploy that upset the routine and distracted Duke. Actually, the lockeroom was next to practice fields and at least a quarter mile walk or more to the stadium. I saw no sense in walking that far to warm-up; walk back in and walk out again. That was the reason. Didn't know it was coaching genius at work.

***

I remember taking Wake Forest to play the Sooners. When we arrived for our Friday workout at the stadium Oklahoma was still in their Friday routine. A reporter with us went in to watch them practice. A few minutes later they cleared. The reporter told me how much bigger they were than us. He said it was really a size mis-match. He was only half right. . . it was only their offensive and defensive backs and linebackers. The really big guys weren't there.

***

Lou Holtz was the coach at North Carolina State my first few years at Wake Forest. In our first two encounters we were dismantled. The third year Lou said that if he lost to Wake he would have to move out of town. We won and he did. Of course, he moved out of town to take an NFL post.

***

I have an ego but I try to act humble; however, I must tell you that while coaching in the Atlantic Coast Conference I was by far the most popular and best liked coach in the ACC. I know this because every time I came on the field the other coaches always looked over, waved a greeting with a big smile. They should have, I was like an annuity for them.

***

The team was popular, too. How do I know? Because everyone wanted us to come to their Homecoming game.

***

The publicity guy at Wake billed us as the "Throw and Go" team. First couple of years it was true and the fans did. They threw up and went home.

***

There is one advantage in being out of the game by half-time. . .it gives the coach two quarters to work on his post game quotes.

***

In the southwest and southeast, when the game was over, I would see the coach walk off the field with two or more state troopers escorting him. Boy! When I went south to coach I fantasized about my escort and my fantasy became real with but one difference. . . my post game escort was two panhandlers and a pick pocket.

***

I worked with a coach who always referred to the prevent defense as the "pervert" defense. After experiencing the negative outcome of the prevent defense on more than one occasion it may be more than a play on words.

***

There we were, ready to go out on the field for the kickoff against Michigan in Ann Arbor. The usual crowd of well over 100,000 in the stands. Our locker rooms were across from each other in the tunnel. A Wolverine assistant told one of ours that it was time to get on the field and the visitors go out first. I received the message and said that there was nothing in the rule book that said visitors show first. No way I was going to be standing on the field when Michigan came out and the roar went up. Exasperated, Michigan headed out. The instant they entered the tunnels so did we. We ran out on the field with them . . . our kids thought 100,000 plus were cheering for them.

***

When you play Oklahoma, every time they score, they have those horses race around the track pulling that little covered wagon. We lost the game big. . .and I felt so guilty. Not about the score. . . we damned near killed the horses.

***

Cowboy Joe, is a paint horse, that Wyoming charges around the field after a score with a cowboy riding it hard. I gave serious thought to having the horse shot with a tranquilizer. In my mind's eye, I could see the touchdown. . the fans ready to cheer Cowboy Joe. . . and there he is: asleep. I think I had the courage to try it, but I feared an overdose.

***

I have a photograph after we played Penn State. Joe Paterno and I are shaking hands. By the expressions on our faces you would be sure that we had won. Sadly, in the background, is the scoreboard. Penn State had a fifty-five next to it. . .I assure you we didn't have fifty-six.

***

I remember one time, after a game, my wife wasn't waiting for me after meeting with the press as she usually did. I assumed she went home with one of the coach's wives. As I was leaving and driving across the stadium parking lot, there was Barbara walking toward the street. I drove up to get her. I stopped the car and about that time a motorcycle cop shot up. He sees a car driving up to a lone woman and investigated. He looked at Barbara and asked if I was bothering her. Her answer, "don't worry, he didn't score this afternoon and he won't score now!"

***

She entered one of those magazine sweepstakes. She told me if she won $25,000 she would split it with me; if she won $1,000,000 she was leaving.

***

When we made an overnight trip we usually attended a movie on Friday night. I would search the paper to find a flick I thought they would enjoy. The players weren't too happy with my choices. The final straw was the night before a big, big game. I picked a picture starring Richard Burton and Rex Harrison. I thought that should be a good one. the movie was about two gay men and was depressing. The captains asked to take over the flick selection; they had enough of my expertise. They were so upset at my selection they pulled off one of our biggest upsets in the next day's game.

***

The program must serve the young people in it; at least that is a hope. I always thought ours did. A glimpse of this as a reality is that we have had eleven younger brothers follow their older siblings into our program. In fact, three times we have had three brothers (no twins) on the team at the same time.

***

Every team has a few kids who think they are bad guys. Those who are on the edge of encounters with the law. In the 60's, I was coaching at a college near a prison that had a football team. We would scrimmage them in the pre-season. Counting the number of players on the entering bus; being given strict instructions about where they could go; guards escorting them to the rest rooms; searching their equipment bags. . .result? Fewer bad guys on the trip home than on the way in.

***

A decade or so later I had a graduate assistant who, as a younger man, had done some really hard time. . .he was able to give players a lecture on living conditions in prison. The line that got attention and changed expressions, "you learn to always sleep and shower with your fanny up against the wall and your hand over your mouth." Today that coach is a high school teacher and coach, working with at risk kids.

***

For some youngsters being on the team is a major socialization experience. For those who never quite fit in, were never accepted by the group, a team can give them that acceptance. If the kid follows the guidelines he is a part of the team. . .he is doing all that is needed to be a part of the team. . .he is doing all that is needed to be a part of the group. There is the possibility that it will be the only group ever to accept him.

***

At Southern Oregon State we worked hard to recruit black players. There was no black community anywhere in near proximity to the college. There was a single black player on the team when we arrived and another recruited with the incoming freshman class.

***

Southern Oregon State was a non-scholarship program. There were other state colleges closer to the state's black populace and it was only practical they would attend college closer to home.

***

Through overt and aggressive effort, after a few years, we managed to have about eighteen percent of our team black. At the time there wasn't a half dozen black women in the school.

***

The point being, regardless of intentions, there are situations and circumstances that can overwhelm intentions.

***

Utah State football gave me some big thrills. We went into the Big Ten to play Wisconsin. They were big favorites. I know we had a very good team but I didn't know how we would stack up against the Big Ten. To add to the pressure, the game was near Chicago, home to my wife and me. Family and friends came to the game. We won 28-0. We had about a dozen players from that team go on to play in the NFL and the Canadian Football League.

***

Another year we headed for the Southeastern Conference to play Kentucky. One of those games where they wanted us for a win and we wanted the money. The local papers regarded us as "the prescription to get Kentucky well!" The lead headline the next morning, "the medicine killed the patient."

***

We received the opening kickoff and drove right down the field. It was fourth and goal at the one yard line. Our QB, a good one, named Tony Adams, who later played for the Kansas City Chiefs and in Canada, turned and called a time out. He came to the sideline and I asked him why he called the time out?

"Coach, thought you might have a play you wanted." My brilliant response, "you got us this far, I have no idea." He said, "don't worry, I got the play." We scored and 50,000 fans gave me credit for the goal line call. Tony completed twenty-six of thirty-four passes as we won 34-6.

***

In the same game we had a nose guard from East Los Angeles named Truitt White. He was quick but not a very big kid. He demoralized the Wildcat center. We decided, with a 26-0 half time lead we would rest Truitt the last part of the third quarter so that he would be fresh for the final quarter pass rush. In our combination, when we rested him we moved our defensive tackle to the nose. He wasn't quick or cute. He was a pummeler. When we put Truitt back in, their center saw him and commented, "Man, am I glad to see you back!"

***

From high school athletics through the pros most programs have sophisticated weight lifting programs. They can have dual objectives. . . to improve athletic performance and to reduce injuries. Two free weight exercises that seems to have a direct correlation with football are the snatch, bringing the weight from the floor to directly overhead in one movement and the other, the clean and jerk; this requires two movements, from the floor to the press position and then from the press position to overhead. Both exercises require concentration and total explosion, using both the legs and upper body.

***

Some on the field advice for a new coach...be sure you do your agility drills and back peddling so as not to get caught in a pile-up; be sure you have your pants double stitched. In this way, if the kids carry you off the field and go in different directions you may be injured but not embarrassed. Don't hug a muddy player and beware a mother's wrath. If you have a bunch of big kids who can't play, drop them from the team. If you aren't winning the fans look at the big guys and think you are stupid for not playing them. Drop all but two. Tell those two anytime you lose a game their job is to carry you off the field. Then the fans will say, "he can't coach a lick, but the kids sure love him."

***

As a coach I never worried about out coaching anyone or being out coached. My premise was to be sure we didn't out coach ourselves. Simply, do we have our players placed properly? What are their talents? What are the skills needed? Do we have enough time to properly practice them? Our emphasis was on performance. . . not theory. Again, what the players can do. . . not all the coaches know.

***

Strength of character and principle can only come from within. External factors may explain, support and encourage. . .but the fortitude to stand by beliefs is within the spirit. Without internal conviction one may be persuaded to take a stance, however, if it isn't the individual's strength of character, then it won't be lived by or worth a battle.

***

Among the advantages of being a senior citizen are telling people what you really think of them; not having to worry about the next job; people hesitate to tell you to "go to hell" because you are close enough to the end that when you go they will feel guilty. But most of all, you can be as immature as you have always been. . .but need not hide it anymore.

***

Volatile and creative people often shoot from the hip. A good subordinate will help to see that the target is hit someplace, or move the target.

***

Early spring, NFL, free agency! That time of year when name players and not so name players switch teams for dollars. Obscene dollars in most cases . . . but that's show biz. Last year's team is not this year's and won't be next year's. It is impossible to build a team; continuity is lost, development of young players is counter-productive. The fan, realistically understand huge bucks are involved, but emotionally the feel betrayed. They, too, like the owners want the Super Bowl today!

***

A great public debate about the need for political campaign reform because the need for dollars is all-consuming and may compromise ethics and integrity. Many collegiate athletic departments are as fervent for raising money as any politico; are they less inclined to be corrupted?

***

Beyond my protestations to the contrary, I embrace technology. "Defects of its virtue," so to speak. Larry King, talk show host related that he was leaving on a trip; his wife and son were seeing him off. As he departed through the gate, the boy's mother told him to wave good-bye to his daddy. The child turned towards the television set in the airport lounge and waved. Maybe a cute story . . . and a telling one.

***

Weather, other people, physical well-being and many other things you can adjust to but not fully control. <u>The only thing you have that you are in complete control of is your attitude.</u> <u>Attitude may not always be easy to control but the power is yours to exercise.</u>

***

There's more to life than football. There is more to football than football. And a significant part of that "more" are some of the very things you need to live a more than football life.

REMINDERS TO CONSIDER
COACH TO PLAYER:
1. Remember you are coaching somebody's child.
2. Don't get the player and person mixed up.
3. Don't challenge a player's dignity.
4. Approach can vary, but policies must be consistent.
5. Be sure player knows his role on the team.
6. Eliminating a player ends a problem but it isn't solved

ASSISTANT COACH:
1. Be loyal to head coach, staff and program.
2. Let head coach know your aspirations.
3. Know your role and what is expected from you.
4. Meet coaches and build your contacts.
5. Be careful of your conduct...who's watching?

COACH TO TEAM:
1. Players need to know what is expected.
2. Honor time lines.
3. Careful evaluation in placement of personnel.
4. Don't commit to anything you won't or can't deliver on.
5. Don't overload the team. Do what players can practice and do.

HEAD COACH:

1. Coaching may be your life. . .maybe not the player's.
2. Don't bad mouth the coach you replaced . . .your next.
3. Give the loyalty you expect.
4. Know your staff's long-term interests and goals.
5. Consider their families in your scheduling.
6. Provide staff with responsibility, authority and recognition.
7. Know your strength and weaknesses and hire to compensate.
8. Know what your goals are.
9. Set program direction and attitude. . .keep the focus.

In this age of battles between races, genders and age groups there comes to mind a poem by James Patrick Kinney, titled <u>The Cold Within</u>. This poem has been a leading page in our players' notebook since I can't remember when. Here it is:

> Six humans trapped by happenstance
> In bleak and bitter cold.
> Each one possessed a stick of wood
> Or so the story's told.
>
> Their dying fire in need of logs
> The first man held his back
> For of the faces round the fire
> He noticed one was black.
>
> The next man looking cross the way
> Saw one not of his church
> And couldn't bring himself to give
> The fire his stick of birch.
>
> The third one sat in tattered clothes.
> He gave his coat a hitch.
> Why should his log be put to use
> To warm the idle rich?

The rich man just sat back and thought
Of the wealth he had in store
And how to keep what he had earned
From the lazy shiftless poor.

The black man's face bespoke revenge
As the fire passed from his sight.
For all he saw in his stick of wood
Was a chance to spite the white.

The last man of his forlorn group
Did naught except for gain.
Giving only to those who gave
Was how he played the game.

Their logs held tight in death's still hands
Was proof of human sin.
They didn't die from the cold without
They died from the cold within.

***

Coaches beware where they have sports information directors. SID's jobs depend upon cultivating the media. If the SID doesn't like the coach or tired of promoting a losing team, a few "off the record" remarks can start the ball rolling to axe the coach.

***

The "hurry up" offense saves time and may disrupt a defense. On occasion it can energize a lanquid offense.

***

In smaller colleges, where we didn't have the budget to commission market potential studies, we did get good advice and help from the business school. On occasion, when needed, we would get a group of graduate students assigned to the study as their graduate project.

The Fifth Down

This extra down is truly appropriate. Away from coaching for eight years I was appointed head coach at the U.S. Coast Guard Academy. But for Lou Saban, I believe I am the oldest guy ever appointed a college head coach. (I prefer "most experienced"). The core staff assembled was all around my age, with a total of 178 years of college and pro coaching experience and five Super Bowl rings. Thought we might be the only coaching staff to be carried on rather than off the field. (Team set a school record for regular season wins and qualified for post-season play).

***

With sporting good companies giving coaches lucrative contracts for wearing their apparel, I was quite upset we didn't hear from the manufacturer of Depends. Why just June Allyson?

***

I didn't achieve all I had dreamed of in coaching, but more than I deserved. Few bad times and fewer bad people. I have been fortunate to be associated with loyal, hardworking coaches who on so many occasions made me look good. I am indebted to a number of people, coaches and others, who helped me and supported me in my pursuits. And, those great young people who were on our teams, who let me enter their lives and improved mine.

***

As the whistle blows on this extra down, I must repeat a line from a poem written by country singer Jimmy Dean: "I'm drinking from my saucer 'cause my cup has overflowed."

***

This I do know: there are only two ways to stop losing, either -

WIN OR QUIT.

***

"Toot, toot!"

KOKORO: Japanese character that symbolizes excellence is achieved only when body, mind, soul and preparation are as one.

Printed in the United States
49487LVS00001B/28